NETWORKING FOR BEGINNERS

An Easy Guide to Learning Computer Network Basics. Take Your First Step, Master Wireless Technology, the OSI Model, IP Subnetting, Routing Protocols, and Internet Essentials

RUSSELL SCOTT

© **Copyright 2019 - All rights reserved**

The content contained within this book may not be reproduced, duplicated or transmitted without direct written permission from the author or the publisher.

Under no circumstances will any blame or legal responsibility be held against the publisher, or author, for any damages, reparation, or monetary loss due to the information contained within this book. Either directly or indirectly.

Legal Notice:

This book is copyright protected. This book is only for personal use. You cannot amend, distribute, sell, use, quote or paraphrase any part, or the content within this book, without the consent of the author or publisher.

Disclaimer Notice:

Please note the information contained within this document is for educational and entertainment purposes only. All effort has been executed to present accurate, up to date, and reliable, complete information. No warranties of any kind are declared or implied. Readers acknowledge that the author is not engaging in the rendering of legal, financial, medical or professional advice. The content within this book has been derived from various sources. Please consult a licensed professional before attempting any techniques outlined in this book.

By reading this document, the reader agrees that under no circumstances is the author responsible for any losses, direct or indirect, which are incurred as a result of the use of information contained within this document, including, but not limited to — errors, omissions, or inaccuracies.

Table of Contents

Introduction 6
Chapter 1: Networking Basics 7
    Computer Network: The Meaning 8
    LAN vs. WAN 8
    Network Infrastructure 11
    Peer-to-Peer vs. Client-Server 13
    Client-Server Network Architecture 13
    Network Devices 14
    Network Speeds 15
    The OSI Model 16
    Roles of Each One of the 7 Layers 18
    The Network Administrator 24
    Collision and Broadcast Domains 24

Chapter 2: Networking Hardware 26
    Host Machines 26
    Network Adapter (Network Interface Card) 27
    Hub 27
    Switch 28
    Router 28
    Modem 29
    Firewall 29

Chapter 3: Network Cabling 31
    Ethernet Cables 32
    Straight-through Cables 35
    Crossover Cables 36
    Rollover Cables 37

Chapter 4: Wireless Technology 38
    Wireless Hardware 39
    SSID 40
    Bluetooth 40
    WiMAX 42
    Radio Frequency Identification 44
    Communications Protocol 45
    Extending Networks With Wi-Fi 46
    Ad Hoc Mode vs. Infrastructure Mode 47

Chapter 5: IP Addressing 50
    What Is the Function of an IP Address? 51
    The Binary Number System 52

Hexadecimal Number System 53
Default Gateway 54
Finding Your IP Address Manually 55
IP Address Configuration 55
DHCP 57
Default IP Address Classes 58

Chapter 6: IP Subnetting 61

Bit Borrowing 63
Determining the Subnet Mask 63
Calculating Host Addresses per Subnet 63
Determining Host Ranges 64
Subnet Masks Changing 65
VLAN 66
IPv4 vs. IPv6 67
Address Depletion 68

Chapter 7: Network Protocols 69

TCP/IP Model 70
Application Layer Protocols 70
Transport Layer Protocols 72
Internet Layer Protocols 73
Link Layer Protocols 74
Frame Relay Protocol 76
Network Address Translation 76
Routing Types 77
Routing Protocols 79
Routing Tables 82
Ports 82

Chapter 8: Internet Essentials 83

Internet History 83
Internet Technical Terms 87
Worldwide Web: Window to the World 89
Leveraging Your Connection to the Web 90
Common Uses of the Web 90
Assessing Internet Service Plans 94
How to Get Internet Connectivity 94

Chapter 9: Virtualization Architecture and Cloud computing 96

Essence of Cloud Computing 96
Characteristics of Cloud Computing 97
Cloud Computing in Practice 98
Virtualization 98
Components of a Server Computer 100
Virtualization Software 100
Three Basic Kinds of Cloud Services 101

Public Clouds vs. Private Clouds 101
Chapter 10: Network Troubleshooting **103**
Hardware Management and Maintenance 103
Network Troubleshooting 106
Hardware Troubleshooting 107
Summary of Network Management 107
Software Troubleshooting 109
Cable Troubleshooting 109
Wireshark Short Guide 109
How Does Wireshark Work? 110
Conclusion **111**

Introduction

In this book, you are certain to get down to an exciting learning undertaking of various networking experience. Particularly, *Networking for Beginners* concisely sets the tempo with an easy-to-understand introduction to the essentials of networking, so you get to know just enough about the LANs and WANs, the OSI model and networking components.

It is also worth noting that the issue of network maintenance and troubleshooting have been significantly covered. There is appreciable coverage on wireless technology, the Internet, and the interesting concept of virtualization in cloud computing. Also, this book introduces the interesting concepts of IP addressing and subnetting that certainly injects a practical touch to the largely theoretical aspect of networking.

Thoroughly researched to meet the current networking and technological needs of learners, *Networking for Beginners* is a highly practical and up-to-date beginners guide to the essentials of through to the very advanced concepts of computer networking. Prepared from a teaching and guidance point of view, the book does not compel readers to have any experience or prior knowledge in the discipline of networking. Readers have the chance to grab the basics of computer networking through to the fundamental concepts of TCP/IP configuration, router basics, network troubleshooting, network security, IP Management as well as virtualization and cloud computing, among other key networking topics. After reading this book, you will have a considerable understanding of different networking protocols and their role in making the networking concept a reality.

Chapter 1:
Networking Basics

Computer networking is a wide discipline that incorporates numerous computing concepts primarily aimed at improving communication and access to limited (yet sharable) computer resources.

In this chapter, we are going to examine the basic concepts of computer networking. Our discussion shall begin by defining a network, after which we will look at network infrastructure, roles of a network administrator, an overview of the different Personal Area Network with a lot of emphasis on LANs and WANs, and an analysis of peer-to-peer networking vs. client-server networking.

To sum it up, we will take a quick glimpse of the various network devices, terminologies, the OSI model, and wrap it up with a brief discussion of collision and broadcast. This chapter is typically a summary of networking fundamentals that prepares us for more of a highly illuminating networking experience in the subsequent chapters.

Computer Network: The Meaning

Computer network is a term that refers to any collection of computers that are linked to one another for communication and sharing of data (and information) and other computing resources. Other resources that network also permits network hosts to share applications, data, and a lot more network resources of hardware nature-file servers and printers, among many other devices.

Computer networks may be distinguished according to size, functionality and even location. However, size is the main criterion with which computer networks are classified.

Classification of networks according leads us to the following common types of networks:

- LANs
- WANs

LAN vs. WAN

LAN means Local Area Network, whereas WAN, in full, means Wide Area Network.

LAN

A LAN refers to any group of computers that are linked to one another in a small area like an office or a small building. In a LAN, two or more computers are connected via communication media like coaxial cables, twisted pair copper cables or fiber-optic cables.

It is easy and less costly to set up a LAN since it can do just fine with inexpensive network hardware such as switches, Ethernet cables, and network adapters. The limited traffic allows for faster transmission of data over LANs.

Besides, LANs are easy to manage since they are set up in a small space. Thus, even security enforcement is also enhanced through closer monitoring of activities within the network's geographical location.

LAN examples include office networks and home-based networks.

Merits of a LAN

LANs have a rather obvious advantage over WANs considering the LANs' small geographical coverage, unlike the Wans that stretch over unlimited geographical coverage.

The following are the pros of a LAN:

- Ease of installation since it involves a small area within which computers can be connected. The limited area of operation amounts to a limited number of networked machines, which makes it a lot easier to set up a LAN.
- Ease of maintenance due to the small network area and few networked computers.
- Ease of security enforcement since also due to the relatively small operating environment and a few networked devices

Limitations of a LAN

The limitations of a LAN can be summarized in one sentence by considering its confinement to limited geographical space and the number of networked machines. Thus, it is agreeable to conclude that LANs' limitation is its inability to accommodate many users, thereby restricting LANs for use within small offices, business settings, learning spaces, and home settings.

WAN

A WAN is a kind of computer network that stretches over large geographical regions- cities, states and even countries. It is bigger than LAN or MAN. It is not restricted to a particular geographical location. It spans over large geographical locations by the use of telephone lines, satellite links or fiber optic cables. The Internet is a perfect example among the existing WANs globally.

WANs are widely embraced for education, government, and business activities.

Examples of WAN

The following examples show just how WANs can connect people limitlessly irrespective of their geographical locations:

- **Mobile Broadband:** 3G or 4G networks are widely serving people in a big region, state or even country.
- **Private Network:** banks create private networks that link different offices established in different locations via a telephone leased line that's obtained from a telecom company.
- **Last Mile:** telecommunication companies offer internet services to thousands of customers in different cities by simply connecting homes, offices and business premises with fiber.

Notably, the Internet is the most conspicuous example of WANs that connects people in all corners of the universe.

Advantages of WANs

- WANs cover large geographical locations reaching out to masses of the human population. The impact of the Internet on people's lives globally sums up the advantages of a wide area network.
- Centralized data. WANs support the centralization of data/information. This eliminates a need for individuals to buy back-up servers for their emails and files.
- Getting updated files. Programmers get updated files within seconds since software work on live servers.
- Quick exchange of messages. WANs use technologies and sophisticated tools that enable a message exchange to happen faster than on most other networks. Communication via Skype and Facebook are two good examples of quick

message exchange, thanks to the Internet, one of the popular WANs in the world.
- WANs allow the sharing of resources and software. It is possible to share hard drives, RAM, and other resources via wide area networks.
- Business without borders. Presently, even people separated by the Pacific can still conduct thriving business without moving an inch from their current location because of the Internet. The world is indeed a global village.
- High bandwidth. The use of leased lines for companies increases bandwidth. This, in turn, increases data transfer rates, thereby increasing the productivity of the company.

Disadvantages of WANs
- Security issues are escalated as the network size increases. Thus, the issue of insecurity is more concern on a WAN than it is on a LAN or MAN.
- High installation cost. Setting a WAN requires the purchase of many costly equipment as well as software applications to manage and administer the network. Routers, switches, and mainframe computers that are needed to serve the network all cost a fortune.
- Network troubleshooting is often a big concern since the network spans large geographical locations.

Network Infrastructure

Network infrastructure entails all the necessary resources that lead to the full functionality of the networking concept. That is to say, in other words, that hardware, software, network protocols, human input, and design functions that lead to effective network operation, management and communication; all these do constitute what is conventionally referred to as network infrastructure. In a nutshell, the following are some of the elements of network infrastructure:

Network software
Network hardware
Network protocols
Network services

The hardware aspect of a computer network allows users to physically link network devices as well as an interface to gain access to the resources of a network. Hardware typically includes the physical components that constitute a computer network. The physical components of a network include host machines (computers); connecting devices (routers, hubs and switches); and other peripherals (printers, wireless modems, network cameras, and file servers, among others).

As far as network software is concerned, a Network Operating System (NOS) emerges as number one on the list. However, depending on the nature of a network, a NOS may not be necessary, particularly in peer-to-peer network arrangement (coming shortly in a different discussion). Besides a NOS, there are numerous software applications that are installed to operate on host machines that network use to perform different tasks on the network.

Network protocols refer to policies and standards that offer details on how network communication takes place. A protocol is a set of conventions, procedures, rules, and regulations that governs the process of network communication. With this in mind, it goes without saying that an understanding of network architecture (which describes the logical arrangement of computers); and the two network models (TCP/IP and OSI) play a crucial role in the comprehension of the entire concept of computer networking.

A computer serves its users with a number of services. The sum total of the network services constitutes the role of the network (network function). Network services include data storage, directory services, email services, file-sharing services, and many more.

In this section, we will discuss peer-to-peer vs. client-server network architectures, the OSI model, network speeds, the role of a network administrator, and collision and broadcast domains.

Peer-to-Peer vs. Client-Server

Peer-to-Peer Network Architecture

In this kind of architecture, all computers are connected to one another. All computers have equal privileges and share the responsibility of data processing on equal terms.

This form of computer network architecture is ideal for small computer networks supporting up to 10 computers.

The architecture does not provide for a server role. Special permissions are granted to each computer through an assignment. Unfortunately, issues do arise when the computer with the resource breaks down or malfunctions.

Merits of Peer-To-Peer Networks

The following are the main advantages of Peer-To-Peer Network Architecture:
- Less costly since there is no dedicated server.
- It's a small network. Thus, setting up and management of the network is largely easy.
- The failure of one machine does not affect the functionality of others. Hence, it is highly reliable.

Demerits of Peer-To-Peer Network Architecture
- Peer-to-peer arrangements lack centralized systems. Thus, there is no mechanism for data backup since all data is dissimilar in different locations.
- There is no managed security-each computer that has to handle its own security.

Client-Server Network Architecture

In this network model, user computers (known as client computers) rely on a central computer (the server) for resource allocation and enforcement of security.

The server handles security, resource, and general network management. On the other, client computers communicate with one another via the central computer/server.

For instance, if the client "A" wishes to send data to client "B," client A must submit a request for permission to the server. The server then answers back by either granting permission to client A or denying them permission to talk to client "B." When the server grants client "A" permission to communicate with client "B." communication can then be initiated by client A to client y instantly or may require to wait for some time.

Pros of Client-Server Network Architecture

- Data backup is achievable with the presence of a centralized system.
- A dedicated server improves the overall performance through proper organization and management of network resources.
- Security enforcement is a notch higher since the central computer administers all shared resources.
- The speed of resource sharing is higher due to orderly request handling.

The Cons of Client-Server Network Architecture

- Dedicated servers are highly expensive. Thus, they render the network quite costly.
- The administration of the network must be handled by skilled personnel only. Unlike peer-to-peer networks that do not need any highly skilled individual to administer, client/server networks require qualified personnel for effective administration.

Network Devices

From a physical perspective, a network can be quite simple-just two computers connected together to move data from one to the other over a simple Ethernet cable. That's not to say, however, that the network will stay simple. For this reason, you should consider every network building block in the initial design even if it is not included in the first phase of implementation.

Even if you are intent on building a home network or small-office network, you ought to anticipate future needs besides those other things intended for purchase and installation without hesitation; either accommodating the need for space, nodes, and wiring right away or building a plan for making the additions and upgrades. Doing so saves time in the long run and may eliminate some frustration when hooking up a new server doesn't mean that switches, routers, or hubs also have to be changed out.

The following list is a good starting point for identifying the necessary networking components:

- Printers
- Database hosts
- Client workstations and PCs
- File servers
- Laptops, notebooks, and handhelds
- Other peripheral hardware:
  - ⇨ Interface devices
  - ⇨ Hard drives
  - ⇨ Network switching and routing components
  - ⇨ Web cameras
  - ⇨ Network and end-user software
  - ⇨ Removable media

Network Speeds

In computer networking, speed and bandwidth are almost interchangeable, but they are not, really. So, what is speed (and bandwidth)?

Whereas network speed is the circuitry bit rate, bandwidth is that "speed," which ends up being used. Thus, speed refers to the theoretical throughput, while bandwidth is the actual throughput.

In a scenario of the internet, we can define speed in the following ways (bandwidth, actually):
- How fast or slow a new connection can be established.
- How long it takes to stream a video content comfortably.
- How fast or it takes to download content from a website.
- How fast or slow it takes a webpage to open.

Bandwidth plays a key role in determining the "speed" of a network. In the world of computer networking, it is not ridiculous to say that bandwidth is a data rate that a network interface (connection).

Ethernet network bandwidth vary immensely from a few megabytes per second (Mbps) to thousands of Mbps. Different Wi-Fi standards define different speeds (bandwidths), as well as other networking technologies.

Numerous factors lead to differences in theoretical and actual network speeds. Some of the factors include:
- Network protocols
- Communication overheads in the diverse networking hardware components
- Operating systems

Importantly, a discussion about network speeds would not be complete without mentioning the term latency. It refers to the time of data transmission from a network host to the server and back. It is measured in milliseconds. It is sometimes considered as a "ping," which should ideally be recorded at 10ms. High latency is feared to cause slowdowns and buffering.

The OSI Model

OSI is, in full, Open System Interconnection. This model offers a description of the way information and data from a software application is transmitted through a physical media to another software application in a totally unrelated computer.

This reference model is made up of seven layers. Each layer has a specific role to play.

The OSI Reference model was born in 1984 by the International Organization (ISO). In modern days, this is taken to be the basic architectural model for inter-computer communication.

In the OSI model, whole tasks are broken down into 7 smaller and manageable chunks. Layers are assigned distinct roles-each layer is assigned a specific task to handle. Also, each layer is sufficiently equipped to handle its tasks independently.

Characteristics of the OSI Model

The OSI model is broadly divided into two layers: upper and lower layers. The upper layers include the following distinct layers:

- Transport
- Presentation
- Application
- Session

The lower layers include the following distinct layers:

- Physical
- Data link
- Network

The upper layer of this model primarily handles issues related to applications. Those issues are executed in the software. The closest layer (or the uppermost) to the user is the application layer. The end-user interacts with a software application just as the application software does.

When a layer is said to be an upper layer, it is said so about another. An upper layer is a layer that lies right above the other one.

The lower layer of this model handles issues of data transport. The implementation of the data link, as well as physical layers, occurs in software and hardware. In this model, the physical layer stands as the lowest layer. It is also the nearest to the physical medium. Primarily, the physical layers provide the necessary information to the physical medium.

Roles of Each One of the 7 Layers

We are going to focus on the functions of the unique layers of the OSI Reference model from the lowest to the uppermost.

Physical Layer

- **Data Transmission:** It defines the mode of transmission between two network devices-whether it is full-duplex, half-duplex or simplex mode.
- **Line Configuration:** It offers a clear definition of the way two or more network devices are physically linked.
- **Signals:** the physical layer determines the nature of signals used to transmit information.
- **Topology:** The physical layer offers a comprehensive definition of the arrangement of network devices.

Data Link Layer

This layer is charged with the task of ensuring error-free data transfer of data frames over the network. It also defines the data format on the network.

The data link layer ensures that there is reliable and efficient communication between network devices. It is responsible for the unique identification of each device that is found on the network.

The data link layer comprises of the following two layers:

1. **Logical link control layer:** It transfers packets to the destination's network layer. Besides, it identifies the specific address of the network layer of the receiver from the packet header. Furthermore, flow control is implemented in this layer.

2. **Media access control layer:** This refers to a link that exists between the physical layer and link control layer. This is what transfers data packets over a network.

The Data Link Layer's Actual Functions

- **Framing:** the data link layer does the translation of the physical layer's raw bit stream into data packets referred to as frames. It adds a header and trailer to the data frame. The header contains both receiver and source addresses.
- **Physical addressing:** The physical addressing layer enjoins a header to the frame. This header has the address of the receiver. The frame is transmitted to the receiver whose address is indicated on the header.
- **Data flow control:** This is the data link layer's primary role. It maintains a constant data rate so that no data is corrupted while in transit.
- **Error control:** This is achieved by the addition of a cyclic redundant check (CRC) on the trailer that is put into the data packet before being sent to the physical layer. In case of any errors, the receiver can request the retransmissions of the corrupted frame.
- **Access control:** This layer determines which of the available network devices is given top priority over the link at a particular moment.

The Network Layer

It is number 3 on the 7 layer OSI Reference model. It handles devices' IP address assignment and keeps track of device location on the network. Based on network conditions, the layers determines the most favorable path for data transfer from sender to receiver. Another condition that is considered in determining the best path is service priority, among others.

These layers are charged with the responsibility of routing and forwarding packets — routers some of the devices on layer 3. The routers are specified in the network layer and are used to offer routing services in a computer internetwork.

Protocols that are used in the routing of network traffic include IPv6 and IP.

Network Layer Functions

- **Addressing:** This layer ensures that the destination and source addresses are added to the header of the frame. Addressing is helpful in the identification of devices on a network.
- **Internetworking:** The network layer offers a logical link between network devices.
- **Packetizing:** The network layer receives frames from the upper layers and turns them into packets in a process that is conventionally referred to as packetizing. It is realized by the Internet protocol.

The Transport Layer

It is the number 4 layer in the model.

The layer ensures that it follows the order in which they are sent. It makes sure that duplication of data does not occur. This layer's core business is to ensure that data is transferred totally.

The physical layer receives data from the upper layers and subdivides them further into smaller chunks that are referred to as segments.

The layer provides communication between destination and source —from end-to-end— for data reliability. It can also be termed as end-to-end layer.

There are two protocols that are implemented at this layer:

- Transmission control protocol
- User datagram protocol

TCP

TCP is a short form of Transmission Control Protocol. It is a standard protocol which allows systems to share messages/information over the internet. The protocol establishes and preserves the link between the hosts.

TCP divides data into smaller units referred to as segments. The resulting segments do not travel over the internet using the same route. They reach the destination in no specific. However, TCP reorders the individual segments at the destination to reconstitute the original message.

User Datagram Protocol (UDP)
It is as well a transport layer protocol. As opposed to TCP, the source does not receive any acknowledgment when the destination receives data. This renders the protocol quite unreliable.

Transport Layer Functions
Whereas the network layer does the transmission of data from one machine to another, it is the transport layer that ensures data transmission to the appropriate processes.

- **Segmentation and reassembly:** This layer receives a message from its upper layer. It then splits the whole message into several small chunks. The layer assigns sequence numbers to each segment for identification.
  At a destination point, the transport layer reconstitutes the segments based on the sequence numbers to form the original message.
- **Service-point addressing:** Service-point addressing enables computers to run multiple applications simultaneously. It also allows data transmission to the receiver not only from one machine to another machine but also from one process to another process. The transport layer adds a port address or service-point address to the packet.
- **Flow control:** This layer also ensures data control. The data control is done from end to end, but not across one dedicated link.
- **Connection control:** there are two services that the transports offer — connectionless service and connection-based.
  A connectionless service considers each segment to be a distinct packet. The packets travel through different routes to the destination. On the other hand, the connection-based service makes a connection with the destination machine's transport for before packets are delivered. In the connection-based service, all packets move on a single route.

- **Error control:** Just like in data control, this is achieved on an end-to-end basis-not across a single link. The transport layer at the source ensures that the message gets to its destination error-free.

The Session Layer

This layer establishes, maintains, and synchronizes the interaction between communicating network devices.

Session Layer Functions

- **Synchronization:** The session layer adds checkpoints in a sequence during data transmission. In case of errors along the way, retransmission of data takes place from the specific checkpoint. The entire process is referred to as synchronization and recovery.
- **Dialog control:** This layer serves as a dialog controller. The layer achieves by initiating dialog between two processes. Alternatively, the layer can be said to authorize communication between one process and another. This can either be half-duplex or full-duplex.

The Presentation Layer

This layer primarily deals with the language and formatting of information that is transferred between two network devices. It is the network's "translator."

The presentation layer is a section of the operating system. It is the portion of the operating system that does the conversation of data from a given presentation format to another presentation format.

This layer is also called the *Syntax Layer*.

Role of the Presentation Layer

The layer does the conversion of data from the sender-based formats into common formats into receiver-dependent formats on the destination computers.

- **Encryption**

    The presentation layer performs encryption to ensure the privacy of data.

Encryption is the process that involves the conversion of information transmitted from the sender into another unique form that is then transmitted over the network.

- **Translation**

    Processes in different systems exchange information as character numbers, character strings, and many more. Different encoding techniques are applied on different computing machines. It is the presentation layer that handles interoperability between them, unlike encoding techniques.

- **Compression**

    The presentation compresses data before its transmission. The compression involves the reduction of the number of bits. This process is essential, especially in the transmission of different multimedia like video and audio files.

The Application Layer

This layer offers the interface for users and applications to access resources on the network. It handles network issues like resource allocation, transparency, and many more. This is not an application. It simply plays its application layer role. It provides network services to end-users.

Role of the Application Layer

- **Access, transfer, and management of files:** This layer allows users to access files remotely, retrieve them, and still manage them remotely.
- **Mail services:** This layer offers an email storage and forwarding storage facility.
- **Directory services:** This layer offers the distributed database bases. This is essential in the provision of important information about different objects.

The Network Administrator

For a network to serve its functions as desired, there's always an individual who's charged with the responsibility of working tirelessly to make the networking experience an interesting affair. That person, normally operating behind the scenes, is known as the network administrator. A network operator ensures that the network is up-to-date and working properly.

A network administrator performs many tasks as a fulfillment of their mandate. In summary, the following are the main tasks that a network administrator has to perform:

- Physical network storage and cloud management.
- Basic testing and security enforcement measures.
- Offering assistance to network architects with network models design work.
- Operating systems and server management.
- Software updating and deployment.
- Network troubleshooting.
- Repair work and upgrade of network.
- Configuration of network software such as switches, routers and servers.

A network administrator must be highly knowledgeable and skilled in IT, particularly in computer networking. They must be able to think critically and possess strong analytical skills so as to handle complex network issues effectively.

Collision and Broadcast Domains

A collision domain refers to the network portion that is vulnerable to network collisions. Collisions take place when two or more network hosts transmit data packets simultaneously on a single network segment. It must be understood that the efficiency of a network deteriorates when collisions occur. Issues of collisions are rampant networks that rely on hubs for connectivity with host machines and other devices. Hub-based networks are prone to collision issues since ports on a hub are in one collision domain. This is not the case when router-based and switched networks.

A broadcast is forwarded in a broadcast. Thus, a broadcast refers to the network segment where a broadcast is relayed.

A broadcast domain is composed of all network devices that communicate at the data link layer via a broadcast. By default, switch and hub ports belong to the same domain. On the contrary, router ports belong to different domains. Also, a router cannot forward a broadcast from a broadcast domain to another.

Chapter 2:
Networking Hardware

Though there are both software and physical network components, our primary focus in this section is channeled towards discussing about the physical components of a computer network. Essentially, physical computer networks include host machines (computers), routers, hubs, switches, repeaters, Network Interface Cards (NICs), network servers, modems, and many other peripheral devices.

Host Machines

Host machines (computers) include desktop computers, laptops as well as portable devices (smartphones and tablets) plus their additional accessories such as portable hard drives, CD Players, keyboards and mice. They are the major hardware components of any computer network.

Computers are the primary components without which a network is just but a dream. Computers offer the platform for users to perform their different tasks on the network. In the case of a centralized system, computers serve as a link between users and the dedicated network server.

Network Adapter (Network Interface Card)

The network adapter or NIC (as it is commonly called) is a hardware component that links one computer to another on the same network.

The NIC supports network transfer rates from 10Mbps through to 1000Mbps.

All network cards have unique addresses assigned by the IEEE. These are referred to as the physical/MAC addresses and are used to identify each computer on the network.

There are two unique forms of network cards:

- **Wireless Network Adapter**

    A wireless NIC comes with an antenna for grabbing a connection over a wireless network. Laptops normally have an inbuilt NIC whereas some desktop computers may require an installation of a separately purchased NIC- fortunately computer motherboard do have NIC slots for the wireless NIC.

- **Wired Network Adapter**

    The wired NIC comes fixed on the motherboard of almost all computers. Connectors and cables are used for data transfer when it comes to wired NICs.

Hub

A hub divides a network connection into several devices. A hub connects all computers on a network via cables. Every computer sends a request to the network through the hub.

When the hub gets a request from a particular computer, it broadcasts that request across the network to all network devices.

Each network device checks the request to determine if it belongs there. If not, the request is subsequently discarded.

The downside to this process is the consumption of more bandwidth and communication is highly limited. Presently, a hub is as good as obsolete due to the hype with routers and switches.

Switch

A switch links a number of devices on a computer network. This important connection device is technologically more advanced than a hub.

A switch has an update that determines the destination of transmitted data. The switch transmits a message to the desired destination as per the physical address on each incoming request.

Unlike the hub, it does not transmit data to all devices across the network. Thus, there are increased data transmission speeds since individual computers communicate directly with the switch.

Router

A router gives an internet connection to a local area network. It receives, analyzes, and forwards incoming packets to another computer network.

It operates at Layer 3 in the OSI model-simply referred to as the network layer.

Packet forwarding is governed by the contents of the routing table. A router is smart enough to choose or decide the most appropriate path for the transmission of data from all available paths.

Benefits of Routers

- There is a high security level of transmitted data/information. Although transmitted data/information traverses an entire cable, it is only a specified device for which the message is intended that reads the data/information.
- It is reliable since the malfunctioning or breaking down of the router only slow down a given network, but any other network which is served by the router is not affected.

- A router increases overall network performance. In case a certain number of devices generate the same amount of traffic on a network, the router has the ability to divide the network further into two equal 'subnets' to reduce the increased traffic.
- Routers allow for a larger network range with little concern over performance issues.

Limitations of Routers

Disadvantages of routers are normally ignored, but we can mention just two:
- The use of routers is a highly costly affair. Routers are highly expensive. They add to the overall cost of a network.
- There is a need for skilled personnel. An inexperienced, unskilled individual cannot administer a network that has a connection with another larger network using a router.

Modem

A modem is an acronym that stands for Modulator/Demodulator. It changes digital data into analog signals over a telephone line.

The modem makes it possible for a computer to establish a connection to the Internet via an existing telephone line. It is installed on the PCI slot of the motherboard-not on the motherboard itself.

Modems are classified as follows based on data transmission rates and different speeds:
- Cable modem
- Dial-Up Modem/Standard PC modem
- Cellular modem

Firewall

A firewall could be in hardware or software form. So, it is in order to define a firewall as a network device or software application that restricts entry into and out of a private network. Private networks are normally connected to the internet. Firewalls come in quite handy when there is a need to restrict network users from gaining unauthorized entry into such networks, especially intranets.

When messages are being transmitted in and out of the internet, they are supposed to pass through the firewall for screening. Those that do not fulfill certain requirements are denied access through the firewall.

It must be noted that firewalls do not offer authentication services besides traffic screening and network connection permissions. Thus, they should be complemented to guarantee enhanced security for networks.

There are a variety of firewalls. They include:

- **Packet-filtering firewalls:** Examine packets that leave or enter a network, and only allow those that meet the permitted threshold.
- **Circuit-level gateway:** Security measures are applicable to the establishment of UDP or TCP connection. The packets flow unchecked once the connection is established.
- **Proxy server firewalls:** The proxy server establishes internet connectivity and submits requests on behalf of a host machine. There is a way in which proxies are configured to filter traffic that passes through them.
- **Web application firewall:** This one enforces a set of rules to HTTP conversations. The rules are customized to identify potential attacks and block them.

Chapter 3:
Network Cabling

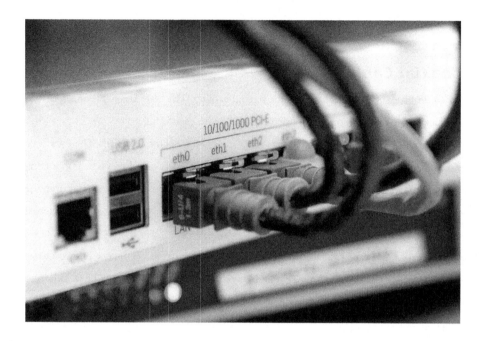

C abling is one of the most crucial aspects of computer networking. The cables provide physical connections between different networking components for interconnection and to serve as communication media. In other words, cabling is used to establish links between network devices besides offering a medium through which packets are transmitted from source to a designated destination.

Cables are classified according to type and function. Popularly, we use Ethernet cables for most networking tasks. In this section, we are going to discuss the following networking cables.

Ethernet Cables

Ethernet cabling entails the use of 3 common cable types. They include:

- Coaxial.
- Twisted pair copper.
- Fiber optic cables.

Coaxial Cables

Often, internet access is achieved with coaxial cabling. The term coaxial is analogous to the fact that it has two conductors that run parallel to each other.

Coaxial cables contain conductors that run through the center of cables. There exists a layer of insulation that surrounds the conductor. In addition, there is a conducting shield that comes right after the insulating material. The insulating material and the conducting shield make coaxial cables highly resistant to interference from the external environment.

Coaxial cables are categorized into thinnet and thicknet types. Thinnet is referred to as Thin Ethernet (10Base2) cable, while Thicknet is referred to as Thick Ethernet (10Base5) cable. They are practically outdated forms of Ethernet cabling techniques.

Thicknet uses Radio Grade 8 coaxial cable with conformation to the specification of original Xerox Ethernet and has a 0.5" diameter. On the other hand, thinnet is a thinner Radio Grade 58-similar to Radio Grade 6 TV cable.

A thicknet supports data rates of up to 10 Mbps and extends to up to 500m of length. This cable standard supports up to 100 devices in a time of one second. Similarly, thinnet supports up to 10Mbps, just like the thicknet. However, it can only extend up to185m (intentionally meant to be 200m) of length. Besides, thinnet can support only up to 30 devices.

The following are the main characteristics of coaxial cables:

- A coaxial cable consists of two conducting materials that run parallel to each other.
- The two conductors include the inner conductor and the outer conductor. The inner conductor is made of single copper wire, whereas the outer conductor is

made of a copper mesh. The two conductors are separated by a non-conductor.
- The middle core is responsible for data transmission, whereas the outer copper mesh is an insulation against electromagnetic interference (EMI).
- Compared to twisted pair cables, coaxial cables have a higher frequency.

Twisted Pair Cabling

A twisted pair cable contains four different copper wires. The wires are twisted around one another. The twisting aims at reducing external interference and crosstalk. This type of cable widely used in many LAN implementations.

Twisted pair cables are used in both network cabling and telephone cabling. They are classified into Unshielded Twisted Pair cables and Shielded Pair Cables. The former are commonly known as UTP cables, whereas the latter are referred to as STP cables.

UTP Cables

UTP cables are commonly embraced for use in telecommunications. They fall into the following categories:
- **Category 1:** This is widely used in low-speed data telephone lines.
- **Category 2:** This one can support data speeds of up to 4Mbps.
- **Category 3:** This one can support data speeds of up to 16Mbps.
- **Category 4:** This one can support data speeds of up to 20Mbps, and can be used for long-distance data transmissions.
- **Category 5:** This one can support data speeds of up to 200Mbps and can even allow data transmission over longer distances as compared to any other of the above categories.

Merits of UTP Cables
- They're relatively cheap.
- They can be efficiently used on implementations of high-speed LANs.
- It is easy to install unshielded twisted pair cables.

Limitation of UTP Cables
- They're limited to short distances since they're prone to attenuation.

Shield Twisted Pair Cables

A shielded twisted pair cable has an insulating mesh that surrounds the conducting copper wire for enhanced data transmissions. They are characterized by the following:
- They are vulnerable to attenuation. Thus, the need for shielding.
- Shielding ensures higher transmission rates of data.
- Shielded twisted pair cables are easy to install.
- There are moderate in cost.
- It accommodates higher data capacities for transmission than the unshielded twisted pair cables.

Limitations of Shielded Twisted Pair Cables
- They are more costly than the Unshielded Twisted Pair cables.
- They are highly prone to attenuation.

Fiber Optic Cable

This is a cable that uses electrical signals for data transmission. The cable holds optical fibers with plastic coating to send data using pulses of light. The plastic coating is highly helpful since it protects fiber optic cable against extreme temperature changes and electromagnetic interference from other electrical connections. Fiber optic transmissions are way faster than coaxial and twisted pair cable transmissions.

Elements of Optic fiber Cable
A fiber optic cable is composed of the jacket, core and cladding.

Core
This may be a narrow strand of plastic or glass for light transmission. The amount of light that passes through the fiber increases with an increase in the size of the core.

Cladding

This refers to the concentric layer of glass. It primarily offers a lower refractive index at the interface of the core to allow the transmission of light waves through the fiber.

Jacket

A jacket is a plastic protective coating for the preservation of the strength of a fiber, offer fiber protection and absorb shock. We will examine the advantages of fiber optic cables over twisted pair copper cables:

- Greater Bandwidth. Fiber optic cables offer higher bandwidth. Thus, they transmit more data than twisted pair copper cables.
- Faster speeds. Fiber optic cables transmit in the form of light signals. This makes optic data transmissions unusually high as compared to transmission via twisted pair copper cables.
- Data transmissions can occur over longer distances than transmission via twisted pair copper cables.
- Fiber optic cables are less prone to attenuation. Thus, they are more reliable than twisted pair cables.
- Fiber optic cables are thinner and stronger than twisted pair copper cables. This makes them enable to withstand more pull pressure than twisted pair copper cables.

Straight-through Cables

A straight-through cable is just another type of twisted pair copper cable that connects a network host (computer) to a router, switch and hub. A straight-through cable is also referred to as a patch cable. A patch cable is another option for a wireless connection in a case where a single or more host machines connect to a router via wireless signal. Pins match on a patch cable. Also, it uses just a single wiring standard at both ends-the T568A or T568B wiring standard.

Crossover Cables

A crossover cable is a form of Ethernet cable that provides direct linking between different networking devices. This cable is also referred to as the RJ45 cable. It uses different wiring standards at its terminal points-T568A at one end and T568B at the other end. A crossover cable's internal wiring reverses receive and transmit signals. It is used to connect similar networking devices. For instance, a crossover cable can be used to connect one computer to another computer, or one switch to another switch.

Summary of Crossover vs. Straight-Through Cables

Primarily, straight-through cables are used to link dissimilar networking devices while crossover cables are used to link similar devices. So, straight-through would come in handy in connecting the following devices:

- Switch to server
- Hub to Computer
- Switch to computer
- Hub to Server
- Switch to Router

Crossovers are necessary for the following networking device connection scenarios:

- Hub to hub
- PC to PC
- Switch to hub
- Switch to switch
- Router to router
- PC NIC to Router Ethernet port NIC

Rollover Cables

Rollover cables are actually "rollover wired cables." They have opposite pin alignments on their terminal ends. That is to say that the first pin on connector A links with pin 8 of connector B. rollover wired cables are also referred to as YOST cables and are primarily used to link to a networking device's console port so that it can be reprogrammed. Whereas crossover and straight-through cables are intended for data transmission, a rollover cable is mainly used to create an interface with a given networking device.

Chapter 4:
Wireless Technology

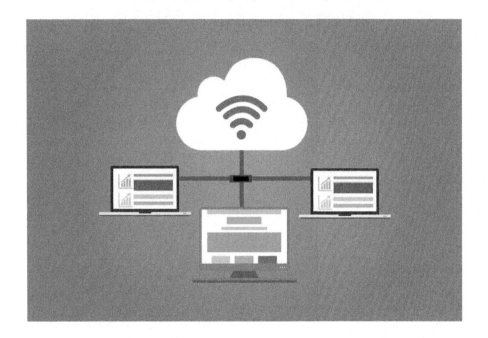

Wireless networking has grown into a full-blown IT discipline since it is apparently a more affordable form of networking, especially when it comes to file sharing, access to digital media, and Internet surfing. With the rapidly growing mobile technology and mushrooming mobile device manufacturing, it is no doubt that wireless networking is, and will continue to take the world years in, years out.

There are advancements in wireless. Most notable is the rise and rise in the development of wireless technologies. In this section, we will stay focused with a clear mind of uncovering the hidden details of the most common wireless technologies in use. Specifically, we will delve deep-deep enough-into the essentials of three wireless technologies: WiMAX, Bluetooth and RFID.

And just before we drown in the discussion of Bluetooth, RFID and WiMAX wireless technologies, we need to stay alert to the fact that wireless is also the most vulnerable to intrusion and hacker attacks. Thus, it is of massive significance to pay attention to the idea that we need to sufficient with regards to wireless network security. In fact, we're going to examine potential wireless network attacks and security threats that play a key role in watering down the integrity of this contemporarily popular 'sub-concept' of the larger networking concept.

Wireless Hardware

It is good to know that a wireless network is not 100% wireless. There are various hardware components that make the wireless concept a reality. The following are the most important hardware components of a wireless network:

- **Wireless NIC:** Wireless network adapters have built-in receivers and transmitters. Once the adapters are installed within respective devices, the devices transmit and receive signals among themselves to achieve communication.
- **Wireless network router:** Wireless router performs the conventional function of a wired router, the only difference being that the wireless router doesn't have a physical connection with other network devices. Other than the packet forwarding function, the router also serves as an access through which users can connect to other network and the internet. Devices that are served by the wireless router must have wireless network adapters.
- **Wireless range extenders**: These are devices that scale the wireless network's coverage. These are also known as range expanders or boosters. They amplify the signal, thereby improving signal quality.
- **Wireless access points:** These are wireless network devices that act as interconnection points. They connect wireless clients to the internet, Ethernet or other wireless access points.

SSID

SSID is a short form for Service Set Identifier. If we know that, in the context of wireless technology, service set refers to a collection of wireless network devices, then we ought to know that SSID refers to the technical name that identifies a given wireless network.

SSIDs are case sensitive names of up to 32 characters. Special characters are admissible when coming up with SSIDs.

A Wi-Fi base (wireless router) broadcasts its SSID allowing Wi-Fi-enabled devices to show a full list of wireless networks within reach. An open network is just connected without a need for authentication. On the other hand, a secured network will request a passkey without which one cannot establish a connection.

Bluetooth

Primarily, Bluetooth came in as an alternative to the issue of heavy cabling that rocked the connection-based mobile phone, computer, fixed electronic device, and an assortment of hand-held device 'networking' needs. Bluetooth is based on the 802.15 IEEE standard. Instead of using cable for data transmission, a 2.4GHZ ISM frequency is instead used for the transmission.

Bluetooth technology offers three power classes of Bluetooth output. The Bluetooth output power classes determine the distance limits within which data transmission can occur. The three output power classes are listed below:

- **Power Class 1:** The maximum output power for this Bluetooth technology class is 20dBm. Data transmission is possible within an operating distance of about 100m.
- **Power Class 2:** The maximum output power for this Bluetooth technology class is 4dBm. Data transmission can occur within an operating distance of about 10m.
- **Power Class 3:** The maximum output power for this Bluetooth technology class is 0dBm. Data transmission can take place within an operating distance of about 1m.

How Does Bluetooth Work?

Enabling a Bluetooth device gives it the power to search for any other available Bluetooth enabled devices within its data transmission range. An enabled Bluetooth device employs an inquiry procedure to discover other enabled Bluetooth devices within its reach.

Once a Bluetooth device is discovered by another Bluetooth device, it relays an inquiry reply back to the Bluetooth device that initiated the inquiry. What follows a successful inquiry reply is the entry of both devices in the paging procedure.

In the paging procedure, the two devices establish and synchronize a connection. The completion of the establishment of a connection between the two Bluetooth devices results in what is referred to as a piconet.

The term piconet refers to an ad hoc network. This network can comprise of up to eight Bluetooth enabled devices. The device may comprise different devices, all of which only require to be Bluetooth-enabled. Computers, earpiece, mobile phone, mouse, and many other devices that support the Bluetooth feature.

Installing a Bluetooth Network Between a Mac OS X and Any Other Bluetooth—Enabled Device

- Click on Apple then go 'Systems Preferences.'
- Click 'Bluetooth' and choose 'Settings' under 'Hardware.'
- Click 'Bluetooth Power' button on the window that pops up to power Bluetooth on.
- To make sure that your Mac OS X device is seen by other Bluetooth within range, click 'Discoverable.'

Choose the Device That You Wish to Connect With

- Select 'Devices' and choose 'Set-up New Device' then choose 'Turn Bluetooth On' in case it is not yet turned on already.

- After the above, 'Bluetooth Setup Assistant' starts to guide you through the selection of your desired.
- There are options of keyboard, other device and mobile phones. Let's go with 'Other Device' in our illustration.
- The Bluetooth Device Setup will begin the search for any other available Bluetooth device that the Mac OS X with which it can establish a connection. When another Bluetooth device shows up, a notification pops up on the screen. If that's the device of your choice, then select 'Continue.' This process is known as pairing.

Bluetooth security may require you to provide a 'passkey.' The 'passkey' limits the number of people who can establish a connection with your device. It is only someone who has the 'passkey' that has authority to establish a link between your device and theirs.

In rather general terms, the following are the essential steps of establishing connectivity between two Bluetooth-enabled devices:
- Locate the Bluetooth button from the device's settings and turn it on.
- Make sure that the devices are discoverable by enabling the 'Discoverable' mode in the Bluetooth settings.
- Select your preferred Bluetooth device for pairing from the list of available devices.

WiMAX

The acronym WiMAX can be broken down as follows:
- W-Worldwide
- I-Interoperability
- M-Microwave
- AX-Access

Thus, WiMAX, in full, is worldwide Interoperability for Microwave Access.

A wireless broadband was primarily created to serve as a broadband wireless access (BWA). It is designed to be used for mobile and fixed stations as a wireless alternative to last mil broadband access. It found in the frequency range of between 2GHz and 66GHz.

Broadband wireless connectivity for fixed network stations can go up to 30 miles. On the other, broadband wireless access for mobile stations lies in the range of 3 to 10 miles.

3.5GHz is the WiMAX frequency standard for the international market. On the other, the WiMAX frequency standard stands at 5.8GHz (unlicensed) and 2.5GHz (licensed).

In addition to the above, there are investigations underway for the use of WiMAX in the 700MHz frequency range.

OFDM is the signaling format for WiMAX. OFDM stands for Orthogonal Frequency Multiplexing Division. This format was chosen for the WiMAX, standard IEEE 802.16a, since it boasts of its enhanced non-line-of-sight, commonly referred to as NLOS features in the frequency range of 2.5GHz to 11GHz.

An Orthogonal Frequency Multiplexing Division system relies heavily on multiple frequencies to transmit from source to destination. This is especially helpful with multipath interference minimization issues.

By using OFDM, a system is capable of sifting out the best frequency for data transmission in cases of interference problems with different frequencies. Besides, WiMAX offers a variety of channel sizes that are adaptable to WiMAX standards around the globe, to ensure maximum data transmission rates. The channel sizes include 3.5GHz, 5GHz and 10GHz. Furthermore, WiMAX (IEEE 802.16a) MAC layer is different from IEEE 802.11 Wi-Fi MAC layer. Unlike Wif-Fi, WiMAX only requires to complete a single entry to obtain network access. The base station allocates a time-space to WiMAX once it obtains entry into a network. Thus, WiMAX is given scheduled network access by the base station.

WiMAX operates in both multipoint and point-to-point arrangements. This is profoundly essential in cases where DSL and cable network access is unavailable. This wireless network technology is also vital in the provision of last mile connection. Besides, it has a distance limit of up to 3o miles.

Radio Frequency Identification

This is commonly referred to as RFID and is a wireless network technology that is employed mostly in the identification and tracking of animals, persons, shipments and objects using radio waves. The technique is based on the modulated backscatter principle. The "backscatter" term simply refers to the reflection of radio waves that strikes the RFID tags. The radio waves, then reflect back to the transmitting source. The stored, inimitable identification information is contained in the reflected radio waves after hitting the RFID tag.

The RFID system is made up of the following two things:
- A reader
- RFID tag

A reader is also known as a transceiver. This is made up of an antenna and a transceiver. The RFID tag is also known as the RF transponder. It consists of radio electronics and an integrated antenna.

The transceiver (reader) relays radio waves that activate the RFID tag. The RFID tag then sends back modulated data with its unique identification information to the transceiver. The transceiver extracts the modulated data sent by the RFID tag.

Features of an RFID System

The following are the three core characteristics of an RFID system:
- Frequency of operation.
- Means of powering the RFID tag.
- A communication Protocol, which also referred to as the air interface protocol.

Powering the RFID Tag

There are three classifications of RFID tags based on how they get the power to operate. The three forms of RFID tags include active, semi-passive and passive.

Active RFID Tags: These tags are battery-powered to stay alive and do the signal transmission back to the transceiver.

Semi-active RFID Tags: The electronics on the tag are battery-powered, but the tags use the "backscatter" principle to transmit the signals to the reader.

Passive RFID Tags: Rectification of the RF energy, that strikes the RFID tag from the reader, is the source of power for the RFID tag. The rectified energy provides enough power to power the electronics on the RFID tag and also transmit the radio signal back to the reader.

Frequency of Operation

RFID tags need to be configured to the transceiver's frequency in order to be get activated. LF, HF and UHF are the three frequencies that RFID tags use.

- **LF**: Low frequency use frequency shift-keying between 125-134GHz.
- **HF**: High frequency use the 13.56GHz industrial band.
- **UHF**: Ultra high frequency work at radio frequencies of between 860 to 960MHz and also at 2.5GHz.

Communications Protocol

Slotted Aloha is the air interface protocol that's adopted for RFID tags. It is quite similar to the Ethernet protocol. The slotted Aloha protocol only allows RFID tags to transmit radio signals at predetermined time intervals after getting powered. This technique greatly minimizes the chances of collisions of RFID transmissions. It also permits the reading of up to 1000 RFID tags in one second.

WAPs even allow users to access the Internet while traveling. For example, someone hangs a special device in their motor home's window. It connects to a port on a computer and, when placed within a modest distance (as close as a few feet through obstructions such as thick walls or as far as 400 or so feet in open air) of an active WAP it will facilitate connections to local area networks and to the Internet. If you are close enough to a WAP to pick up the signal, and the signal from your wireless access device is adequately strong and reliable, you can easily connect.

Extending Networks With Wi-Fi

Most often, when someone talks about *wireless networking*, they are referring to the use of one or more Wi-Fi standards.

These include the following standards, which are most prevalent with home and small-office networks:

- 802.11g
- 802.11b
- 802.11n draft

These standards collectively, although a bit complex, can essentially be thought of as standards that allow for Ethernet networking without the wires. The standards vary in how they operate at the medium (radio wave) level; for the end-user, the most notable difference is the throughput speeds. The 802.11n standard, for example, uses more than one radio transmitter and receiver to increase the throughput of data.

Although wireless networks will probably never replace wired ones—the security, simplicity, reliability, and consistent data speeds available through wired networks will keep them as a viable connection methodology well into the foreseeable future—they do provide a viable alternative to wired networks for small offices and home networks with a minimal number of nodes. Indeed, some network implementations eschew the use of wires altogether, relying only on a wireless network for connectivity. In other implementations, wireless networks provide supplemental connectivity. In addition, publicly accessible WAPs, called *hot spots*, frequently found in fast-food restaurants, coffee shops, hotels, and airports, enable mobile workers and travelers to connect and stay in touch.

Note

With wired networks, the term "at wire speeds" is interpreted to mean the data is passing through the network at a rate that is dictated by the physical limits of the devices and wires comprising that network. In wired networks, connecting a computer to a Fast Ethernet (100Mbps) or a Gigabit-speed (1,000Mbps) network does not guarantee that that processed throughput will equal those speeds. Speed limiters in a wired environment include the wire itself, the performance of the network interface card (NIC), and the bus speed of the computer's system board and processor. Similarly, wireless networks have a carrier radio frequency that, under the various standards, is designed to carry data under ideal conditions at the rated data throughput. Your actual throughput, however, will be less for all the same reasons as wired networks — plus the fact that the signals are affected by distance and by radio interference from other nearby wireless networks, portable phones, and even microwave ovens. If you are using a Wi-Fi device that should get, for example, 11Mbps throughput, it probably won't in a typical environment.

Ad Hoc Mode vs. Infrastructure Mode

Ad Hoc Mode refers to a wireless networking mode in which wireless operates in a peer-to-peer arrangement without centralized administration using a device such as a router. Data forwarding takes place directly among the devices connected to the ad hoc network.

Ad hoc networks require simple and quite minimal configuration and are easily deployed. They are, therefore, ideal when a small, temporary LAN is needed, or a cheap and all-wireless LAN implementation.

To set up an ad hoc network, there is a need to configure respective wireless adapters to use in ad hoc mode. Also, the devices on the ad hoc network must use the same SSID and channel number.

Infrastructure Mode

In infrastructure mode, all devices on a wireless network communicate via a central access point. The access point is often a wireless router. Devices transmit packets to the access point, which then forwards the packets to their intended destinations.

Wireless Network Security

Wireless networks are quite vulnerable to attacks. Primarily, wireless signals sometimes extend beyond their intended geographical limits, making it quite difficult to restrict access, especially to those who are intent on intruding into the network.

Security Threats

Essentially, the following are the common threats to wireless networks:

"Parking Lot" Attack

Due to the dispersion of wireless signals from access points to areas where they're not intended, wireless networks are easy prey for intruders. In parking lot attacks, intruders would simply hang around outside an organization (like in a parking area); to take advantage of the wireless signal that spreads beyond the organization's perimeters. They can easily hack the network and gain access to the internal network resources and cause interference.

Shared Authentication Flaw

Attackers can exploit shared authentication through passive attacks. They may eavesdrop on the challenge and response between the authenticating client and the access point. The attacker may capture the authentication information and use it to access the network. This attack can be prevented via encryption of data between clients and the access point.

Service Set Identifier Flaw

When devices are not reconfigured, attackers could use the devices' default SSIDs to gain access to the network. Configuration of network devices to change device SSIDs is a preventive measure against such attacks.

Vulnerability of WEP Protocol

Wireless devices that enforce WEP for security enforcement on wireless networks are prone to eavesdropping since such devices WEP is disabled by default. It is, therefore, advisable to change device settings to customized setting that are not easily predictable.

Chapter 5:
IP Addressing

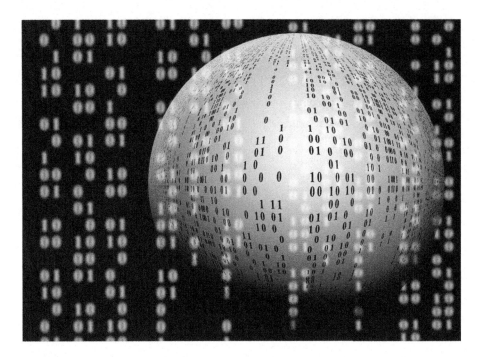

An IP address is a four-octet, eight-bit digital address (32 bits total) that, when written out, looks appears as follows: 10.156.158.12. Evidently, an IP is a special set of numbers that are separated by dots. The set of numbers is used to identify a computer (or network device) using Internet Protocol (IP) for network communication. In an IP address, the value of any of the octets —the numbers between the periods— can be from 0 to 255.

An IP address is not entirely different from a phone number. If you know someone's phone number-say, your Uncle Brown-you can call her by dialing her number on your telephone's keypad. Then, your phone company's computers and switching equipment go to work to connect your phone with the phone belonging to Uncle Brown over an audio communication channel.

Once connected, you can speak with Mr. Bradley, even if he is many miles away. When you do, the audio signal carrying your voice will typically travel over a pair of copper wires from your house to a switch at your local phone company.

From there, the signal might be converted to a light wave in order to travel over a fiber optic cable to another switch. From this second switch, the audio signal might be converted to a radio-wave signal in order to travel from one microwave tower to another. Eventually, as the signal nears its destination—Uncle Mike's house—It will be converted back to an analog audio signal, traveling over a pair of copper wires from Uncle Brown's phone company in her house. (This scenario assumes the use of land lines. If cell phones are involved, then this process will vary in the details, but not in the concept.)

What Is the Function of an IP Address?

In a similar fashion to how phones use numbers to connect on a local, regional, national, or international scale, an IP address facilitates connections between computer hosts as well as routing equipment. Put another way, if two computers on the Internet have each other's IP address, they can communicate. But unlike phones, which use switching equipment to connect, computers connect to each other over the Internet through the use of routing equipment, which shares the communication paths with hundreds or thousands of other computers.

When data is relayed from a computer to a router, the router's job is to find a short, open communication path to another router that is both close to and connected to the destination computer.

The router accomplishes this either by using default routes or by dynamically learning and recording tables, called "routing tables," that keep track of which IP addresses are present on any one of the router's many open, up and running communication ports. Because all the routers connected together on the Internet resemble a spider's web, data can travel over many different routes or paths if necessary to get to its intended destination. If one of the routers or some other connecting link goes offline, the other routers try to move the data search for an alternative route to the destination.

In order to facilitate this dynamic communication method, routers also assign IP addresses so they can find each other.

The Binary Number System

Before diving into the details of how binary works, let's begin with first looking defining (or actually describe) what a binary system is, and its essence in computing terms.

So, what do we mean by a binary number system?

This is a base-2 number system. This kind of number system was invented by one Gottfried Leibniz. The base-2 number system, analogous to the name, is composed of merely two numbers, 0 and 1, and forms the basis for each and every bit of binary code. As we all know (or ought to know), binary code is the only machine readable code for all computer systems.

Binary in Action

The electrical ON and OFF signals are represented by 1 and 0, respectively. When one adds 1 to 1, they typically move the 1 a spot to the left into the 2's place. They then put the 0 into the 1's place. The outcome is 10. So, unlike in the decimal number system where 10 is equal to ten, a 10 represents 2 in the base-2 number system.

If we consider the popular decimal number system, place values begin with 1s and move steadily to 10s, 100s and 1000s towards the left. This is typical as a result of the decimal system's basis upon the powers of 10.

Similarly, place values in the binary number system begin with 1s to 2s, 4s, 8s and 16s leftwards, in that order. This is simply because the binary system operates with powers of 2. The binary digits, 0 and 1, are referred to as bits.

Essence of Binary Number System

Computers are electric powered, and the circuitry is constantly in ON/OFF switching mode. This means that computing devices are able to operate more efficiently with ON/OFF electric circuit switching mechanisms to represent numbers, letters and other characters.

Hexadecimal Number System

We've talked about the decimal number system being base-10 number system and the binary number being base-2. So, as the name suggests-and going by what we've already looked at, it is not inaccurate to conclude that the hexadecimal number system is a base-16 number system.

The hexadecimal number system operates with 10 numeric numbers and 6 non-numeric symbols. Thus, it is made up of 16 'symbols.' Since there are single-digit numerical values after 9, the first letters of the English alphabet are used, namely A, B, C, D, E, and F.

Hexadecimal	Decimal value
A	10
B	11
C	12
D	13
E	14
F	15

How Hexadecimal Works

A nibble represents a hexadecimal digit—a 4-bit value. The digit is represented by any of 0-9 or A-F symbols. When two nibbles are summed up, we obtain an 8-digit value that is known as a byte. Commonly, computer operations are based on bytes. Thus, it becomes much more effective to represent such large values using a hexadecimal representation than a binary representation of numbers. For the sake of bringing down chances of minimizing confusion, it is important to terminate or start hexadecimal representations with "H" or "0x." For instance, h34, ox605, 45h, or anything in that format.

Default Gateway

A default gateway refers to a network node that uses the IP suite to act as a router that forwards packets to a computer in on a different network unless there exists another path specification which matches the IP address of the receiving network host.

Finding the IP Address of the Default Gateway

It is important to be able to know the IP address of the network's default for effective troubleshooting and to gain access to web-based management of a router. Normally, the router's private IP address is the default gateway's IP address. It is the IP address with which a router communicates with another local network. However, the private IP address may not necessarily be the default gateway's IP address, so you need to find it in some way.

The following is a step-by-step guide on how you can find the IP address of the default gateway (for all Ms. Windows versions):

1. Firstly, open the Control Panel.
2. Secondly, select Network and Internet (in Windows XP, you will have to click on Network and Internet Connections).
3. The next step is to click on Network and Sharing Center (if using Windows XP, click Network Connections and skip step 4 and hop to 5).
4. Select Change Adapter setting in the Network Sharing Center (or Manage Network Connection if you are using Windows Vista).
5. Trace the default gateway's IP connection.
6. Double-click network connection. This opens Wi-Fi Status, Ethernet Status or just another dialog (it depends on which network you're using).
7. Select Details (or Support tab, then Details in Windows XP).
8. Locate IPv4 Default Gateway, Default Gateway or IPv6 Default Gateway.
9. The Default Gateway's IP address ought to appear in the Value Column.
10. Note the Default gateway's IP address.

11. You can now use the IP address of the default gateway to troubleshoot connection issues in the network; access the router, or perform any other function thereon.

Finding Your IP Address Manually

It is sometimes important to know the IP address of your machine. Below is a simple way of finding what IP address is assigned to your machine:

- Open the CMD prompt by clicking on Start->Run, then type cmd and press the ENTER key.
- Type the command ipconfig/all in the command that opens in step 1.

You should see a window that shows the IP addresses of your computer, DNS servers, default gateway, and subnet mask, among many more important aspects of the network. Alternatively, you can consider doing the following:
Ping the IP address of the router (assuming that you know it). To ping the IP address of the router, open the command prompt (like in the first method).

Exercise: What appears in the CMD prompt should tell you whether your machine is properly configured with an IP address or not.

IP Address Configuration

The following is a step-by-step guide on configuring the computers in our office LAN:

When Working With Windows 8/10

- Open Control Panel
- Choose Network and Internet
- Click on Network and Sharing Center
- Click on Local Area Connection
- Select Properties

➢ Click Continue (Local area connection properties window opens)

On the Local Area Connection Properties Window

➢ Double-click on TCP/IPv4 (opens properties menu)
➢ Select Use the following IP address from the Properties menu
➢ Enter the IP address and subnet mask
➢ Click OK

When Working With Windows 7

➢ Click Start
➢ Go to Control Panel
➢ Choose Network and Internet
➢ Select Network and Sharing Center
➢ Click Local Area Connection
➢ Select Properties
➢ Click Continue (Local Area Connection Properties windows opens)
➢ Double-click TCP/IPv4 (Properties menu opens)
➢ Select Use the following IP address
➢ Enter the IP address and the subnet mask
➢ Click OK

The process is more or less the same in other Windows operating system versions, with quite little differences.

In Mac OS:

➢ Click Apple
➢ Click System Preferences
➢ Click Network
➢ Click Network Status

- ➢ Select Built-in Ethernet
- ➢ New screen appears with Configure IPv4 option
- ➢ Select Manually
- ➢ Set IP address and subnet mask (manually)
- ➢ Select Apply

In the configuration of the above office LAN, subnet mask 255.255.0.0 is used (do further reading to know more about subnet masks).

DHCP

DHCP is the short form of Dynamic Host Configuration Protocol. This is a protocol that provides swift, automatic and centralized IP address allocation in a network. DHCP is also used in the proper configuration of the default gateway, subnet mask and DNS server.

DHCP in Action

We now know what the DHCP does. But we do not know how it does whatever it does. Trust me, we won't get out of here without a proper understanding of how DHCP performs its functions.

DHCP Server

A DHCP server issues unique IP addresses and constructs other network information automatically. Whereas small businesses and homes rely on routers to perform the functions of a DHCP server, the implementations of large networks could make use of a single dedicated computer to do the same work.

Clients on routed networks request for IP addresses from the routers. Routers respond by assigning available IP addresses to the network devices that sent their requests.

Requesting devices must be turned on and connected to the network. The request must be directed at the server. Such a request is known as a DHCPDISCOVER request. The DHCPDISCOVER request is contained in the DISCOVER packet. The server responds by providing the client an IP address with a DHCPOFFER packet. The network device then responds by accepting the offer. If the server finds it suitable to confirm the IP address assigned to the device, it sends an ACK that the device indeed has been assigned a given IP address. If the server finds it unsuitable to confirm the assignment of IP address to the device, it sends a NACK.

Merits of Using DHCP

- The use of DHCP eliminates the chances of assigning the same IP to more than one network device.
- Dynamic IP address allocation makes network management quite easy, from an administrative point of view.

Demerit of Using DHCP

- Each computer or device on the network must be configured appropriately so as to be assigned an IP address by the DHCP server (and communicate on the network).
- The ever-changing IP addresses for stationary devices such as printers are unnecessary since other devices that are connected to such devices have to constantly update their settings for synchronization.

Default IP Address Classes

There are quite many IP address classes in the IP hierarchy. The IPv4 addressing system identifies five different classes of IP addresses.

The classes are listed below:
- Class A Addresses
- Class B Addresses
- Class C Addresses
- Class D Addresses
- Class E Addresses

Class A Address

This class of IP addresses is characterized by the following key features:

- The initial bit of each first octet of a Class A network address is always set to zero. Thus, the first octet of a network address lies in the range of between 1 and 127.
- A class A address only includes IP addresses beginning with 1.x.x.x up to 126.x.x.x.
- Loop-back IP addresses are taken care of in the IP range of 127.x.x.x.
- The default subnet mask of Class A addresses is 255.0.0.0. Thus, the class A Address network can only accommodate 126 networks.
- The format of Class A IP addressing is given as
0NNNNNNN.HHHHHHHH.HHHHHHHH.HHHHHHHH.

Class B Address

This class of IP addresses is characterized by the following key features:

- In a class B address, the initial two bits of the first octet are always set to one and zero.
- IP addresses of Class B type range from 128.x.x.x to 191.255.x.x.
- Class B's default subnet mask is 255.255.x.x.
- Network addresses in Class B are given as 2^{14} (16384).
- There are 65534 host addresses per network.
- The IP address format for Class B is
10NNNNNN.NNNNNNNN.HHHHHHHH.HHHHHHHH

Class C Address

Class C address is characterized by the following features:

- The first three bits of the network address first octet are always set to 110.
- IP addresses of Class B range from 192.0.0.0 x to 223.255.255.255.
- Class C's default subnet mask is given as 255.255.255.x.

- Class C boasts of 2^{21} (2097152) network addresses.
- There are 2^8-2 (254) host addresses per network.
- The format of Class C address is given as
110NNNNN.NNNNNNNN.NNNNNNNN.HHHHHHHH

Class D Address

Class D addresses have the following features:
- The first octet of the IP address contains 1110 as its first four bits.
- IP addresses of Class D range from 224.0.0.0 to 239.255.255.255.
- This class is reserved for multicasting. Multicasting involves the transmission of data, not to one host or two, but to multiple hosts. This is the reason why it is unnecessary to extract host addresses from the IP addresses of class D. there is also no subnet mask for Class D.

Class E Address

The following are the features of Class E:
- IP address in Class E is set aside for R&D, study or experimental functions only.
- IP addresses in this class range from 240.0.0.0 to 255.255.255.254. Just like Class D, Class also doesn't have a subnet mask.

Chapter 6:
IP Subnetting

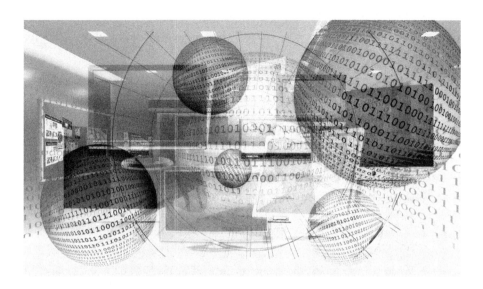

Routed IP environments require that your pool of IP addresses be subnetted. This allows each subnet to see itself as a discrete segment of the larger internetwork. The router then ties together the various subnets into one network. The router knows how to route traffic to the correct segment because it builds a routing table. The routing table is basically the networks' roadmap.

IP subnetting is fairly complex, and so to make this discussion informative, but still digestible at an introductory level, we will limit our exploration of subnetting to one class of IP addresses; we consider the illustration of subnetting a Class B range of IP addresses. The mathematical tricks that we use to subnet the Class B network can also be used to subnet a Class A or Class C network (although subnetting Class C networks greatly limit the number of usable IP addresses that you end up with).

Subnetting is a two-part process. First, you must determine the subnet mask for the network (it will be different than the default subnet masks; for example, the default for

Class B is 255.255.0.0). After figuring out the new subnet mask for the network, you must then compute the range of IP addresses that will be in each subnet.

Okay, let's chat a little before we do the math of subnetting a Class B network. I think it will aid in the overall understanding of the subnetting process. The following is a simple description which shows the new subnet masks, the number of subnets, and the number of hosts per subnet that would be created when using a certain number of bits for subnetting:

- When we use 2 bits, the subnet mask is 255.255.192.0; 3 is the number of subnets; and there are 16382 hosts per subnet.
- When we use 3 bits, the subnet mask is 255.255.224.0; 6 is the number of subnets; and there are 8190 hosts per subnet.
- When we use 4 bits, the subnet mask is 255.255.240.0; 14 is the number of subnets; and 4094 is the number of hosts per subnet.
- When we use 5 bits, the subnet mask is 255.255.248.0; 30 is the number of subnets; and 2046 is the number of hosts per subnet.
- When we use 6 bits, the subnet mask is 255.255.252.0; 62 is the number of subnets; and 1022 is the number of hosts per subnet.
- When we use 7 bits, the subnet mask is 255.255.254.0; 126 is the number of subnets; 510 is the number of hosts per subnet.
- When we use 8 bits, the subnet mask is 255.255.255.0; 254 is the number of subnets; and 254 is the number of hosts per subnet.

Given 130.1.0.0 as our Class B network, 130.1 represents our designated network. The first and second zeros represent the third and fourth octets, respectively. The third and fourth octets are reserved for the host addresses. We have to borrow bits from the third octet to create class B subnets. Keep in mind that the more bits borrowed, the more subnets we create, but fewer host addresses (as is evident in the above description of Class B subnetting). Also, the network ID section of the IP address is fixed.

Bit Borrowing

Suppose we needed to come up with 30 subnets from our 130.1.0.0 network; we would have to first compute the bits that ought to be borrowed to come up with the subnet mask.

To know the number of bits, we have to get the sum of lower order bits, then subtract one (since we can't use subnet 0).

The ordered bits are 128, 64, 32, 16, 8, 4, 2, and 1.

Lower ordered are counted from 1, 2, 4... whereas higher ordered bits are counted from 128, 64, 16...

So, 30 subnets are obtained by getting the sum of 1+2+4+8+16 minus 1.

Which is 31-1=30.

Counting from 1 to 16 (1, 2, 4, 8, 16) gives us 5 bits.

So the number of borrowed bits is 5.

Determining the Subnet Mask

From the above subnetting description, our subnet mask is certainly 255.255.248.0. But how do we obtain this figure?

First, we add 5 higher ordered bits to get the third octet of the subnet mask (128+64+32+8+4=248)

Since the default subnet mask is 255.255.255.0, and considering that 5 bits were borrowed from the third octet (third octet value is 255) then, we get our subnet mask as follows 255.255.(128+64+32+16+8+4).0 which gives us 255.255.248.0 as our subnet mask.

Calculating Host Addresses per Subnet

Remember:

Right from the outset of our subnetting endeavor, we settled on 30 subnets for our 130.1.0.0 network. We then borrowed 5 bits from the third octet. Considering that the network ID (130.1) is untouchable, we only had 16 bits for host addresses (sum of bits from the third and fourth octets, each with 8 bits) at the outset. But we borrowed 5 bits from the third octet leaving with just 3 bits. Thus, we're only left with 3 bits from the third octet and 8 bits from the fourth octet. Adding the third octet and fourth octet bits (3+8) gives us 11 bits available for host addresses.

To calculate the number of host addresses, we use the formula:

$$2^x - 2;$$

Where x is the number of available host addresses (11).

So, this leads us to

$$2^x - 2 = 2^{11} - 2;$$

$$2048 - 2 = 246.$$

Therefore, the number of hosts for each of our subnets is 2046.

Determining Host Ranges

Up to this point we have:

- 130.1.0.0 as our network.
- 255.255.248.0 as our subnet mask.
- 30 subnets.
- 2046 hosts per subnet.

To get us going, we'll need to revisit that procedure for determining our subnet mask. We used the higher ordered bits to determine the value of the third octet of our subnet mask.

Can you remember the lowest of the higher ordered bits? Certainly, you do—just like I do. It was 8. So, we go with this lowest of the higher ordered bits as an increment on the third octet of our network address to obtain the first subnet ID and keep doing this all the way to the last 30 subnets.

Thus, the first subnet and subsequent subnets will be as follows:

130.1.8.1 to 130.1.15.254;

130.1.16.1 to 130.1.15.254;

130.1.24.1 to 130.1.15.254;

etc, etc.

Note:

You can neither have a zero (0) in the last portion of an address nor 255 at the end of an address.

Subnet Masks Changing

The subnet mask on every one of the gadgets in a subnet MUST be the equivalent, or you can keep running into certain issues with what they will or won't perceive. It makes a difference not if the mask is 255.255.255.0 or 255.255.0.0 or 255.0.0.0; what is significant is that every one of the machines in that subnet have a similar cover.

All switches and doors must have their ports arranged to coordinate the subnet that they are connected to by means of that port.

You can have various masks in various subnets however, you need a switch or door with two addressable ports, one on each subnet, which is designed for each subnet.

Despite the fact that subnet covers are normally set to separate at every byte point, they can be set to isolate inside a byte; however, this is more enthusiastically to work out as it must be done depending on the twofold figures inside the byte.

Every one of the a subnet cover does characterize what number of hosts the system sees as having a place with it, and after that enables them to talk promptly to one another yet demands whatever else must go to a portal.

You can utilize any IP address extend that you need inside gave that you have a type of door among you and the Internet and use Network Address Translation (NAT) in that entryway. Else you need to apply for and get an open IP address class permit to suit your system. Better to set up a switch or passage with NAT and simply utilize the IP address allotted by your ISP.

Three explicit location gatherings have been saved exclusively for inner use. It is suggested that you utilize these as the Internet switches, and so on are set up NOT to advance on location inside these extents, subsequently, if any traffic gets out coincidentally, it gets dumped at the main switch.

VLAN

VLAN, in full, is Virtual Local Area Network (normally referred as Virtual LAN). It refers to a switched network that is segmented logically using a project team, application or function. The logical segmentation is done without consideration of users' physical locations.

VLANs are more or less the same as physical LANs. The only difference is that VLANs allow end stations to be grouped regardless of whether they are on the same physical segment or not.

A VLAN can accommodate any form of switch module port. Multicast, broadcast, and unicast data packets can be relayed and swamped to end stations only in a given VLAN. Each VLAN is taken as a logical network. Packets fated for stations outside of a VLAN must be forwarded through a router to reach its destination. Notably, a VLAN can be associated with an IP subnets.

Supported VLANs

Conventionally, we identify VLANs with numbers ranging from 1 to 4094.

The following must be noted:

- 1002-1005 VLAN IDs are set aside for FDDI and Token Ring VLANs.
- VLAN IDs > 1005 are not found in the VLAN database since they are extended-range.
- Switch module supports extended-range and normal-range VLANs (1005).
- The number of configured features, SVIs, and routed ports affect the functioning of the switch module hardware.

VLAN Configuration Guidelines

It is important to understand the following facts:

- 1005 VLANs are supported on the switch module.
- Numbers between 1 and 1001 are used to identify normal-range VLANs.
- 1002 -1005 are reserved for FDDI and Token Ring VLANs.
- Switch module has no FDDI and Token Ring support.
- 1-1005 VLAN IDs are normally stored in the VLAN database, as well as the file containing the switch module configuration information.
- 1006-4094 (extended-range) VLAN IDs are limited to private LAN, RSPAN VLAN, MTU, and UNI-ENI VLANs. These VLAN IDs are not kept in the VLAN database.

The following steps will help you create or modify a VLAN:
1. Use the [configure terminal] command to enter the global configuration mode.
2. Enter the [vlan <*vlan-id*>] to enter VLAN configuration mode.
   Use an existing VLAN ID to modify an existing VLAN.
   Choose a new ID to create a new VLAN.
3. Use the command [name <*vlan-name*>] to give your VLAN a name.
   Though, this is optional for normal-range VLANs.
4. Use the [mtu <*mtu-size*>] to set the MTU size.
   This is also optional.
5. Use the command [end] to return to privileged EXEC mode.
6. Use the [show vlan {name *vlan-name* | id *vlan-id*}].
7. Use the [copy running-config startup config] command to verify entries.
8. To delete a VLAN, use the command [no vlan *vlan-id*].

Note that VLAN 1 and VLANs 1002-1005 cannot be scrapped.

IPv4 vs. IPv6

Currently, IP version 4 (IPv4) addresses are the Internet IP addresses of choice. As mentioned, these addresses are composed of four sets of eight bits. In the future, we will likely adopt the IP version 6 (IPv6) address scheme. IPv6 differs in form and substance from IPv4 in two ways:

- IPv6 addresses have eight 16-bit numbers (128 bits total), usually expressed in four-digit hexadecimal form. The range of a single 16-bit number is greater than that of an eight-bit number, spanning from zero to 65,535.
- The 16-bit numbers in an IPv6 address are separated by colons rather than periods.

Why make the switch? Because under IPv4, there are not enough numbers available to assign one to every computer or device on the Internet that needs one. IPv6 solves this problem, offering 2 raised to the 128th power addresses; in contrast, IPv6 offers only 2 raised to the 32nd power-although masking, and private-address strategies have been used to extend the number of available IPv4 addresses on the Internet.

Address Depletion

IP address depletion refers to the exhaustion of unassigned IPv4 addresses. The IP address has always been anticipated considering the unchecked upsurge in computing devices, high-speed growth of the internet, and limited IPv4 IP addresses. The deployment of IPv6 was a response to the IP address depletion scare as a result of the apparent IPv4 limitations.

Further, a number of concepts have been established to address the same issue while still implementing IPv4 IP addressing. Most popular of the responses to IP address depletion was the concept of the Network Address Translation and the Classless Inter-Domain Routing (shortened to CIDR).

Chapter 7:
Network Protocols

Every worthwhile pursuit is only accomplished when there is a set of rules and regulations and a step-by-step procedure that ought to follow strictly. The networking concept's success has been thanks to the constant initiatives of refinement of the networking working environment through improvements of architectures and networking models.

Network protocols refer to networking rules and regulations that assure the efficiency of networking functions. The network services are attainable due to the existence of network protocols. Consistency of networking standards is sustainable thanks to network protocols.

Given different models (precisely two network models), it is no doubt that we're certainly expected to encounter dissimilarities in the implementation of the networking concept. Thus, the implementation of TCP/IP and OSI network models shows appreciable variations-notably, in respect of network protocols applied. In this section, we'll channel our focus towards an understanding of network protocols found at each layer of the TCP/IP model.

TCP/IP Model

This model came into being way before the conception of the OSI model. The TCP/IP model exhibits remarkable differences from the OSI model. Essentially, the TCP/IP model is made up of 4 layers that are listed below (from the lowest to the highest layer):

- The network access.
- The internet.
- The transport.
- The application layers.

There are different network protocols typical to each of the aforementioned layers. Each protocol performs a specific role, thereby contributing to the total functionality of a particular layer. The sum total of the four layer functions completes the networking concept's primary role of connecting devices, sharing of resources and facilitating network communication.

Application Layer Protocols

This is the uppermost layer in the TCP/IP model. It is also referred to as the process layer. It handles issues of representation as well as high-level protocols. The layer permits interaction between the user and applications.
When an application layer protocol wishes to have some communication with a different application layer, it sends its message to the transport layer.

Not all applications can be installed in the application layer. It is only those applications that interact with the communication system that can be placed inside the application layer.

For instance, a text-editor can never be installed in the application, but a web browser that uses HTTP can be placed in the application layer. This is because the browser interacts with the network directly. HTTP must be noted as an application layer protocol.

Hypertext Transfer Protocol: It allows users to gain access to data that is available on the worldwide web (www).

HTTP transfers data as plain text, video and audio. It is referred to as Hypertext transfer protocol since it can efficiently use hypertext environment characterized by rapid shifts from one document to another.

Besides, HTTPS also works in this layer. It is a pampered version of HTTP. HTTPS means HTTP with SSL (Secure Socket Layer).

HTTPS is most ideal where browsers require form-filling, authentication, and for bank transactions.

Simple Network Management Protocol (or simply SNMP): This is a framework that's important for device management on the internet. It uses the TCP/IP protocol suite.

Simple Mail Transfer Protocol (or simply SMTP): This is a TCP/IP protocol that supports e-mail services. The sending of messages from e-mail to another is made possible by the SMTP.

Domain Name System (or simply DNS): The connection of a host machine on the Internet is identified by the use of a unique IP address that is assigned to each host.

People prefer the use of names to IP addresses since it is easier to deal with names than addresses. For this reason, the DNS is used to map names to different addresses.

File Transfer Protocol (FTP): This is a standard internet protocol that is used for the transmission of files in a network-from one machine to another.

Terminal Network (TELNET): This protocol establishes a connection between a local machine and another remote machine so that the local terminal seems like a terminal at the remote end.

Other protocols present in this layer include the following:

1. Secure Shell (SSH).
2. Network Time Protocol (NTP).
3. X Window, among many others.

Transport Layer Protocols

This layer is analogous to the OSI model's transport layer. It ensures end-to-end communication between hosts. It also has the responsibility of ensuring error-free data delivery.

The transport layer protects the application layer from data complexities. The main protocols available in this layer are as follows:

User Datagram Protocol (UDP): this is the cheaper alternative of the TCP. This protocol does not provide any of the TCP's features. This means that UDP is a less effective protocol, but does have less overhead. As a result, it's less costly as compared to the TCP.

UDP is an ideal protocol in situations where reliable transport is not a priority. It is a cost effective option. UDP is a connectionless protocol, unlike TCP which is connection-oriented.

Transmission Control Protocol: this layer ensures reliable and error-free end-to-end communication between hosts.

This layer handles data segmentation and sequencing. Furthermore, the transmission control protocol has the highly valuable acknowledgement and controls data flows using flow control mechanisms.

In spite of this layer being so effective, it carries a lot of overhead due to the aforementioned features. The more the overhead, the higher the implementation, and vice-versa.

Internet Layer Protocols

The internet layer's functions run parallel to the functions of the OSI model's network layer. Protocol definition occurs at the internet layer. These protocols are responsible for logical data transmission over a whole network.

The main protocols available at the internet layer include the following:

IP Protocol: This protocol is responsible for the delivery of data packets to the destination host from the destination host. The layer achieves this by checking for IP addresses that are found on the packet headers.

IP has 2 versions that include IPv4 and IPv6. Most websites rely on IPv4. However, the use of IPv6 is growing steadily since IPv4 addresses are limited in number, whereas IPv6 are not limited in number when compared to the numbers of users.

Internet Control Message protocol (or simply ICMP): This protocol is encapsulated within datagrams. It is charged with the responsibility of the provision of information about network issues to the network hosts.

Address Resolution Protocol (ARP): this protocol is charged with the identification of host addresses using familiar IP addresses.

There are several types of ARP: Proxy ARP, Reverse ARP, Inverse ARP and Gratuitous ARP.

Link Layer Protocols

The link layer (network access layer) corresponds to the OSI model's combination of the physical layer and data link layer. This layer checks out for hardware addressing. The protocols present in the network access layer permits data to be transmitted physically.

Ethernet Protocol: Presently, the most widely used LAN technology is Ethernet. The Ethernet protocol operates in the link layer of the TCP/IP network model (and in both the physical and data link layers of the OSI model).
Ethernet protocol relies on Logical Link Control (LLC) and MAC sub-layers of TCP/IP's Link Layer. Whereas the LLC deals with communication between lower and upper layers, the MAC sub-layer handles media access and data encapsulation functions.

Token Ring Protocol: This protocol requires that the network topology defines the order of data transmissions by host machines. All network hosts are linked to one another in one ring.
Token ring protocol uses a token (a 3-byte frame) that moves around the ring via token passing mechanism. Frames, too, move around the ring in the same direction as the token to their respective destinations.

FDDI protocol: FDDI stands for Fiber Distributed Data Interface. It refers to the ISO and ANSI standards that govern data transmission on fiber optic media in LANs. The fiber optic lines are restricted to a range of up to 124 miles (200km).
The FDDI protocol works in a similar way as the token ring protocol. FDDI is often deployed on the backbone for WANs.
The FDDI networks have two token rings:
- The primary ring that offers a capacity of 100Mbps.
- The secondary ring that acts as a backup in case of failure on the part of the primary ring.

X.25 Protocol: The X.25 protocol suite is typically designed for the implementation of WANs that support packet-switched communications. The X.25 protocol was conceived way back in the 1970s, but only embraced significantly in the 80s.

The protocol suite is presently on high demand for ATM and credit card verification purposely. With X.25 protocol, a single physical line can be used by a multiplicity of logical channels. The protocol also allows the exchange of data between terminals that have different communication rates.

The X.25 protocol suite is composed of the following 4 layers:

Physical layer: This layer outline the electrical, functional, and physical features that connect a computer to a terminal node (packet-switched). The linking is made possible by the X.21 physical implementer.

Data link layer: Data exchange over the link is done by the data link layer's link access procedures. Control information is attached to packets and transmitted over the link. The packets originate from the packet layer. When the control information is attached to the packets, Link Access Procedure Balanced (LAPB) is formed. This kind of services offers a means of delivering a bit-oriented, ordered and error-free frames.

Packet layer: This layer gives a proper definition of data packet format and control procedures for data packet transmission.

An external virtual circuit service is offered by this layer. Virtual circuits come in two forms:

- **Permanent virtual circuit:** This is assigned by the network and is fixed.
- **Virtual call circuit:** The establishment of a virtual call is done automatically via a set up procedure when needed. It is terminated via a call-clearing procedure.

The equipment used in the implementation of X.25 concept includes the following:
- Data Terminal Equipment (DTE).
- Data Circuit Terminating Equipment (DCTE).
- X.21 implementer

Frame Relay Protocol

Frame relay is also a packet-switched communication service. It runs from LANs to WANs and backbone networks. It has two layers, namely:
- Data link layer
- Physical layer

Frame relay implements all standard protocols at the physical layer and is often applied at the data link layer.

Virtual circuits can join one router to multiple remote networks. Often, permanent virtual circuits make such connectivity a reality. Switched virtual circuits can be used as well.

Frame relay is based on the X.25, and a fast packet technology. Data transmission is done through the encapsulation of packets into multiple sized frames. A lack of error-detection is the primarily the cause of the service's high transmission rate. End points perform error-correction functions as well as retransmissions of dropped frames.

The following are the frame relay devices:
- Data Circuiting Terminating Equipment
- Data Terminating Equipment

Network Address Translation

Network address translation (NAT) is an important feature on Internet connection devices and gateways that allows a computer to have an IP addresses that is not visible on the Internet, yet still receive and send data packets over the Internet. These addresses are hidden, and are assigned from a different set of IP addresses-called private IP addresses-from the addresses that are seen or exposed on the Internet. These private addresses are assigned to computers inside the firewall, enabling them to use TCP/IP protocols for communicating to internal devices and to hosts on the Internet without being seen-thereby making it harder to hack into the internal computer. Using NAT is the first tier in firewalling or protecting your network computers from unwanted intruders anywhere on the Internet.

Private IP addresses also extend the connectivity of the Internet to more computers than there are available IP addresses because the same private, internal network IP address can be used at hundreds, thousands, or even millions of locations.

It works like this: When you open a browser to reach, for example, Yahoo.com, the data packet reaches your Internet gateway/firewall, which in turn starts a session to keep track of your MAC address and IP address.

It then replaces your private IP address from the data packet with its own visible IP address in the data packet and sends the request to Yahoo.com. When the information is returned from Yahoo for your session, the process is reversed; the Internet gateway/firewall strips out its own IP address, re-inserts your computer's private IP address and MAC address into the packet header, and passes the packet down the network wire to your computer.

When this happens, your internal IP address is said to have been "network address translated"-although a better term might be "network address substituted." By default, most home network gateways use NAT and assign private IP addresses to all the computers on the home network.

Routing Types

Routing appears in the following classifications:

Static Routing

This is also referred to as non-adaptive routing. The administrator has to add routes in the routing table manually. Packets are sent from source to destination along a path that's defined by the administrator. Routing does not depend on network topology or network state. It is the job of the administrator to decide the routes along which data are transmitted from source to destination.

Merits of Static Routing
- There is no overhead on router CPU usage.
- There is more security since the administrator has control over a particular network only.
- There is no bandwidth usage between different routers.

Demerits of Static Routing
- It is quite exhausting to come up with a routing table for a big network.
- The administrator must be highly knowledgeable in networking, and particularly in the network topology he or she's dealing with.

Default Routing

In this technique, router configuration is done in a way that a router sends all data packets to a single hop. It does not matter the network on which the hop is found. Packets are simply relayed to the machine on which it configured by default.

This technique is most ideal when a given network has to handle a single exit point. However, a router would choose another path that is specified in a routing table and ignore the one that's set by default.

Dynamic Routing

This is also referred to as adaptive routing. In this approach, a router determines the routing path as per the prevailing conditions in the network.

Dynamic protocols the heavy-lifting when it comes to discovering of new routes. These protocols are RIP and OSPF. Automatic adjustments are meant when particular routes fails to function as expected.

Characteristics of Dynamic Protocols
The following are features of dynamic protocols:
- Routers must have the same protocols to exchange routes.

- A router broadcasts information to all connected routers in whenever it discovers an issue or issues in the topology or network status.

Pros of Dynamic Routing
- They're quite easy to configure.
- It's the best option when it comes to determining the best paths due to changes in network status and topology.

Cons of Dynamic Routing
- It's a lot more costly when it comes to bandwidth and CPU usage.
- It's not as secure as default and static routing.

Important:
- A router filters out network traffic not merely by packet address, but by a specific protocol.
- A router does not divide a network physically. It does so logically.
- IP routers divides networks into a number of subnets to ensure that specific network traffic meant for a particular IP address can be allowed to pass between specified network segments. However, this intelligent data forwarding leads to decreased speeds.

Network efficiency is higher with the use of routers in complex networks.

Routing Protocols

Routes that are determined via routing protocols are known as dynamic routes—the configuration of routing protocols on routers aids in routing information exchange.
Let's examine the great benefits that come with routing protocols.
- They eliminate the manual configuration of routers. These are profoundly time-saving and a big relief to network administrators.

- Link failure or changes in network topology do not hinder packet transmission.

Types of Routing Protocols

Two types of routing protocols exist. They are listed below:
- Link state protocols
- Distance vector protocols

Link state and distance vector protocols are collectively referred to as Interior Routing Protocols (IGP), and are used for information exchange within self-governing systems. Border Gateway Protocol (BGP) is an exterior example of Exterior Routing Protocol (EGP) that helps in the routing information exchange between autonomous systems that are found on the internet. Other than the above protocols, there is Cisco's EIGRP protocol. Though it is essentially an advanced form of the distance vector protocol, some descriptions portray it as a product of distance vector and link state protocols.

Distance Vector Protocols

Analogous to the name, the best path is determined by examining the shortest of the routes (distances).

A distance vector protocol relays an entire routing table to a directly linked router with the same routing protocol (the directly linked table is known as a neighbor). Good examples of distance vector protocols are EIGRP and RIP.

Link State Protocols

Just like distance vector protocols, link state protocols perform the same role- determination of the best path for packet transmission. However, their mode of function is different. Instead of sending out the whole routing table to neighbors, link state protocols send out information regarding the network topology so that eventually all the routers with the same protocols have matching topology databases.

All routers executing link state protocols come up with 3 distinct routing tables:

1. **Topology table**: this table contains the entire network topology
2. **Neighbor table**: this table contains information regarding neighbors that implement the same protocol.
3. **Routing table**: this table contains all the best routes for packet transmission.

Link state routing protocols include IS-IS and OSPF protocols.

Summary

Though link state routing protocols and distance vector routing protocols aim at accomplishing the same objective, their implementations are clearly unlike. The following are the obvious distinctions between link state routing protocols and distance vector protocols:

- Distance vector protocols advertise the entire routing table information to the neighbors, whereas link state routing protocols advertise network topology information to neighbors.
- Distance vector protocols show slow convergence, whereas link state routing protocols show fast convergence.
- Distance protocols sometimes update the routing table information using broadcasts. On the other hand, link state routing protocols use multicasts at all times to update the link state routing information to neighbors.
- Distance vector protocols are relatively easy to configure as compared to link state routing protocols.

Samples of distance vector routing protocols include IGRIP and RIP. Link state routing protocols include IS-IS and OSPF protocols.

Routing Tables

A set of rules that often presented in table format for the determination of the best route for packet forwarding by a router or switch is referred to as a routing table. A basic routing table is characterized by the following features:

- **Destination:** This is the destination's IP address for which data packets lands ultimately.
- **Next hop:** This refers to the IP address of the device (not necessarily the final destination) to which packets need to be forwarded.
- **Metric:** This refers to a cost value that is assigned the available route so that the route with the least cost is taken as the best path.
- **Interface:** This refers to the interface of the outgoing network that a network device ought to use for packet forwarding to the destination or next hop.
- **Routes:** This is information regarding direct and indirect subnet information, and default routes to use when there crucial information is lacking or for certain forms of traffic.

The administration of routing tables can either be manual or dynamic. A network administrator performs changes to routing tables of static network devices manually. In dynamic routing, protocols enable network devices to build and maintain routing tables dynamically.

Ports

A network port refers to an application-specific or process-specific software construct which acts as an endpoint. A port is used by transport layer protocols of the IP suite, including TCP and UDP.

Every network port is identified by a port number. A port number associates the IP address and nature of transport protocol over which communication takes place.

Port numbers are 16-bit unsigned integers. Port numbers begin from 0 to 65535.

Chapter 8:
Internet Essentials

This section covers some of the basic technology concepts that make the Internet work and discuss various options for connecting to the information superhighway so that everyone on your network can surf the Internet, communicate via e-mail, share digital pictures with others, conduct research using countless online resources, make purchases online, download movies and music, video conference, and more. To begin with, let's talk a little bit about the history of the Internet

Internet History

When talking about the historical backdrop of any medium, regardless of whether print, broadcasting or the Internet, there are a few issues of strategy. Presumably, the most evident red herring for any type of innovative historicism is the thing that used to be known as the *'incredible man'* hypothesis of history. While this overwhelmed more established types of historiography, which continued by posting lords and commanders, it has been expelled, or if nothing else uprooted from general verifiable records by social and financial investigations, and would have all the earmarks of being less significant to media history. Regardless, the enticement still exists to stamp out the pioneers of any innovation, their Gutenbergs, Bells, and Marconis. While anecdotal subtleties have their significance as a nexus of recorded and material conditions, to seclude an individual 'virtuoso' from mechanical, financial, and social relations misshapes any record of starting points more than it lights up. In the event that the Net as we probably are aware it would not have taken its present structure without figures, for example, Paul Baran or Tim Berners-Lee, it couldn't have been considered without the virus war and monetary goals of the PC business.

The following issue confronting media history, especially when managing the Internet, is progressively unpretentious, yet considerably more dangerous. Innovative determinism, in any event in its solid structure, accepts that the chronicled advancement of a medium is a procedure of vital *'laws,'* whereby the improvement of another medium makes the conditions for social and mental collaborations. Figuring appears to be particularly helpless against this type of determinism, especially since the articulation of *'Moore's Law,'* generally deciphered to imply that PC power will twofold at regular intervals or somewhere in the vicinity—In spite of the fact that, as we will see, taking this individual law outside the realm of relevance creates its own issues.

While speculations of innovative determinism can be valuable for getting away from the humanistic propensity to put people at the focal point of history, one uncommon model being Manuel de Landa's War in the Age of Intelligent Machines (1991), and such a view doesn't evacuate the fraudulent inclination to consider the to be of innovation as one of inborn advancement. A lucid record of mechanical history that exhibits a portion of the ideals and indecencies of such determinism is Paul Levinson's Soft Edge (1997).

As Gary Chapman comments, value-based or deterministic models of mechanical history are a lot less fortunate than those that consider social and material conditions, especially the readiness of governments, organizations and markets to put resources into new media. *'PCs, as different machines, are material portrayals of a long procedure of advancement, mistake, improvement, more blunder, greater improvement, combination of highlights, the annihilation of supplanted rehearses, scholarly achievements and impasses, etc., all encapsulated in the physical item and the manner in which we use it'* (1994:304).

Patrice Flichy has mentioned a comparative objective fact with reference to radio and different interchanges media, that *'what shows up today as a progression of normally enunciated advances seems to be, as a general rule, the historical backdrop of a troublesome section starting with one space then onto the next'* (1995: 100). As to another socially significant advancement, TV, Raymond Williams has contended against the lack of innovative determinism, or *'symptomatic advances'* expelled from social structures: such developments are included not from a *'solitary occasion or arrangement of occasions'*, however depend for their acknowledgment *'on creations made with different closures basically in view'* (1989:13).

Specifically, notes Williams—innovations—for example, telecommunication or power, required an adjustment in social recognitions before they were viewed as valuable.

Similarly, as with the PC, in the previous couple of years the Internet has been allowed an ancient times, the purported *'Victorian Internet'* of the broadcast, which was introduced with Samuel Morse's transmission of the main electric transmit message, *'What hath God created?'* in 1844. Over the next decades, broadcast lines were introduced crosswise over North America and Europe, and in 1866, the primary transoceanic link was laid.

As transmit connections spread over the world, enlarged by phone lines following Alexander Graham Bell's development in 1876, the establishments were laid for a worldwide broadcast communications framework (Moschovitis et al. 1999; Standage 1998).

The advancement of such a framework was helped by the creation of the electronic PC. Despite the fact that Charles Babbage, baffled by the issues of figuring in what Doron Swade has called *'a time of evaluation'* (2000), had planned and incompletely assembled his Difference Motor in the mid nineteenth century, it was not until the mid-twentieth century that the guideline of a universally handy PC —ready to peruse, compose, store and procedure information— was set up.

Alan Turing, who had gone to King's College, Cambridge, and Princeton University, set up the guideline of a mechanical PC, the *'Turing Machine,'* in his paper *'On Computable Numbers.'* Fundamentally, Turing likewise contended that only one out of every odd numerical issue was resolvable and that there are a few issues for which no calculation exists that could be nourished into a PC. In any case, most issues, when changed over into a progression of computerized groupings of 1s and 0s, could be bolstered into a machine by tape, recorded and unraveled for yield.

While Turing was delineating the hypothetical standards of the PC during the 1930s, Konrad Zuse built the primary crude electronic PCs, the Z1 and Z2; the Z1, started in 1936, utilized mechanical entryways to tally parallel numbers (Zuse having picked doubles over decimals since they could be figured all the more rapidly).

In the Z2, these doors were supplanted by quicker electromagnetic transfers, of the sort utilized in phone trades, however, it was not until the development of the Z3 in 1941 that Zuse finished a completely working, programmable PC. Most gadgets of this time were actually close to ascertaining machines. The capacity to process and perform various capacities didn't start until the innovation of the Z3 and other completely programmable, electronic gadgets. ENIAC (Electronic Numerical Integrator and Calculator), housed at the University of Pennsylvania toward the part of the bargain World War, and the Colossus, worked at Bletchley Park in 1943 and intended to figure out codes created by the German Enigma machine.

These early gadgets, which were joined in 1944 by Howard Aiken's and IBM's Mark I and the Manchester *'Child'* in 1948, were enormous machines. ENIAC, for instance, secured 650 square feet, while the Mark I gauged five tons, and such early, immense PCs were loaded up with flighty vacuum cylinders and transfers (the term bug is followed back to a story that one of the main software engineers, Grace Murray Hopper, found a moth in the Mark II in 1947). Just because, in any case, they spoke to the capability of consistently expanding PC control.

The UNIVAC (Universal Automatic Computer), in view of the thoughts of John Von Neumann, was the principal financially accessible PC and the main such machine to store information on a tape. The following undertaking was to discover something to do with this power, and a few analysts have even recommended that the mid-twentieth century insanity for concentrating data owes all around to the development of these behemoths in government and enormous partnerships. All through the 1950s and 1960s, centralized computers, for example, the System/360, alongside the substantially more dominant 'supercomputers,' ruled open reasoning and involved gigantic cupboards in uncommonly cooled rooms gone to via seasoned technocrats.

Internet Technical Terms

Just as you don't necessarily need to know the inner works of a combustion engine to drive a car, it's not imperative that you understand every aspect of how the Internet works in order to take advantage of all that it offers. That said, it never hurts to examine, however briefly, the various terms and concepts that relate to the Internet.

TCP/IP

TCP/IP—short for Transmission Control Protocol/Internet Protocol — is a group of rules called protocols that define how devices, be they similar or diverse (i.e., computers, routers, and modems), connect and communicate with each other. (In this context, a "protocol" describes technical details about how any two communication devices will interact and work together to move digital data from one device to another.)

TCP/IP works by determining the best available transmission path for data to travel. Rather than sending all the data in one large chunk, however, the protocol breaks the data into small packets.

These packets can travel over any number of different paths to reach their destination; when they arrive, they are reassembled in order.

To ensure that packets arrive at the correct destination, each one contains both the destination address and the source address. This information is stored in each packet's "envelope" or "header."

The TCP part of the protocol controls the breakdown of data on the sending end and its reassembly on the receiving end, while IP handles the routing of the data packets.

Think of it this way: Sending data via TCP/IP is not unlike sending letters via the U.S. Postal

Service. Each letter you send by post encompasses the dispatcher's address (i.e., the source address) and the recipient's address (i.e., the destination address). The difference is that with snail mail, you send the whole letter in one package or envelope (packet). If you were to send that same letter over the Internet, it would be sent in hundreds if not thousands of packets (envelopes) to get to its destination, after which it would be electronically reassembled.

Internet protocols in use under the TCP/IP banner include UDP, PPP, SLIP, VoIP, and FTP.

DNS

Just as it is easier to remember someone's name than it is to remember her phone number, so, too, is it easier to remember the location of a Web site by its domain name rather than its IP address. For example, suppose you frequently visit the Web site of Ford Motor Company. Chances are, you will probably remember the site's domain name-i.e., Ford.com-and not its IP address. Your computer's Web browser, however, operates in the exact opposite way. It needs to know Ford.com IP address in order to connect with the site.

That's the point domain name system comes in. When you enter the domain name of a site you want to visit (Ford.com), your Web browser initiates a session with a DNS server either locally or on the Internet to locate the IP address associated with that domain name. DNS servers perform a hierarchical lookup for the IP addresses using domain name associations for registered domain names to locate the IP address of the site you want to visit. If the DNS server your computer is linked to cannot determine the IP address linked with the domain name you entered, the DNS server will then look up the number on successively higher-level DNS servers until it finds the entry (or errors out).

Once the IP address is found, your computer can locate and communicate with the computer housing the Ford.com Web site. The first DNS server stores the association in memory for a time in case you or someone else it serves needs to visit that site again. The DNS server stores only frequently used associations because it can look up the ones it does not know on the higher level DNS servers.

DNS Root Servers

The DNS is administered in a hierarchical manner using zones (managed areas). The highest zone is the root zone. DNS rooters are name-servers operating in the root zone. DNS root servers have the power to respond directly to record queries for data stored in the root zone. They can also refer queries to the right top-level domain servers (TLD servers). TLD servers are level below the root servers hierarchically.

Subnet Mask

A subnet mask is a number applied within a host configuration file that allows for the division of an IP class C network into separately routable networks. For home networks on an ISP's larger network, the subnet mask will most often be 255.255.255.0, because home networks are not usually split into physically separate segments with internal routers. In office buildings and business environments, subnets are used to detach traffic onto physically isolated networks to retain the data traffic on the low and to enhance performance for access to peripherals and local servers. Data traffic destined for another subnet or to the WAN will have to pass through the router.

Worldwide Web: Window to the World

Like a living creature, the Web is relentlessly shifting as networks are added or changed. The evolution of the Internet both in geographic scope and audience offers every linked object with prospects to communicate like never before. If your use of the Web is limited to simply downloading information and receiving e-mail, you are hardly scratching the surface of what can be accomplished over the Web. Ways to use the Web to inform, educate, and exchange ideas, goods, and services with a worldwide audience are limited only by one's imagination and creativity. This chapter merely skims the surface of what you can do on the Web.

Leveraging Your Connection to the Web

Connecting your network—or a subnetwork of your network—to the Internet stretches the reach of your home or office network to the far corners of the earth. For under $120 per month in most markets around the country, you can obtain a connection to the Internet that runs at decent speeds and includes up to five static IP addresses.

These addresses can significantly enhance your ability to garner the most benefit from your connection to the Internet. That's because in order to make Web servers, Webcams, and other resources available on the Web, you need at least one static IP address that is visible on the Internet. Additionally, a static IP address can be used to enable VPN clients to connect to your network resources. Without a static IP address, much of your communication to the outside world is limited. With a static IP address, however, your network can become a Web site, client-services provider, radio station, TV station, or blog—just to name a few.

The Web really is a window on the world. Not only can you see out, obtaining incredible amounts of data from the Web, so too can others anywhere in the world see in, enabling you to share information of your choosing with a worldwide audience. Adding your own resources to the Web-the ultimate unfettered two-way, free-speech forum-can both provide value to you and your organization and increase the utility of the Web for others.

Common Uses of the Web

The following are the main uses of the web:

Finding or Publishing Information

Most people use the Internet to obtain information-which is why some people call it the largest library in the world. The best way to obtain information online is to enter keywords or phrases into a search engine like Yahoo, Google and Ask.

When you type a keyword or phrase into the search field on any one of these sites, it returns any number of links to Web pages that relate to the word or phrase you entered.

Ask yourself or your organization's management: What information about you, your family, or your company should be posted to a Web server?

There is more to getting your information found or your voice heard on the Internet than simply getting a domain name such as thisismywebsite.com. To ensure that the information on your site can be found when someone performs a related search, you enter key search words into your document headings and possibly pay to register your site with various search engines. Learning key search words and adapting your document headings and labels accordingly is a science in itself. And even if you master it, your business Web site might be listed at the top of the search results one day and slip to 100 or 1,000 the next. Like the Wild West, there are few rules on the Internet, and anything goes when it comes to getting noticed.

Communication

This takes place in the following ways:

E-mail

The most popular Internet communication tool is e-mail-that is, messages are sent electronically from sender to host on the Internet, potentially forwarded to other hosts, and ultimately downloaded at the recipient's convenience.

One way to obtain an e-mail account is from your Internet service provider (ISP); most plans include the use of at least one e-mail address. Alternatively, you might run your own home or office e-mail server under a domain name you own. You access messages received via these accounts through special software called an e-mail client.

Another option is to use any one of several free Web browser–accessible e-mail services, such as the following:

- Yahoo! Mail (http://mail.yahoo.com)
- Gmail (http://www.gmail.com)

Instant Messaging (IM)

Another way to communicate over the Internet is via instant messaging (IM). IM provides instant communication; there is no middleman to store or forward the message. Both end-users must be online to IM; when they do, the text they type is transmitted instantly from one to the other in back-and-forth fashion the second the Send button (or similar) is clicked. You can IM using an IM client on your desktop or, in some cases, a Web browser. Popular instant-messaging applications include the following:

- Yahoo! Messenger
- Window Live Messenger

Video Conferencing

Video conferencing gives users the rare chance of conducting virtual meetings, thereby cutting down on a lot of transport costs. To do a video conference via the Internet, at least one participant ought to have a static IP address detectible to the Internet. Moreover, each contributor should have a service with an upload speed of at least 400Kbps to sustain quality communications, principally if you're using the video component. To video conference, you must have access to a Webcam of some sort.

Blogging

Blogs, short for Weblogs, are sites on which people can share information with other interested or likeminded individuals. Think of a blog as a digital journal that can be read by people around the world.

Entertainment and Media

The Internet boasts a plethora of entertainment options, including the following:

- Interactive gaming
- Music
- Video
- News

- Internet radio
- Internet television

Engaging in Commerce

Commerce represents one of the most common uses of the Internet. Business-related activities include (but are not restricted to) the following:

- Retail sales and marketing
- Banking
- Auctions
- Advertising

Downloading Software

Many major software publishers—including Microsoft, Corel, and Sun—offer users the ability to download what would otherwise be boxed commercial off-the-shelf software (COTS). All you need is a good Internet connection and a PayPal account, credit card, or in some cases, a checkbook to pay the fee. There is also a wide variety of trial software, freeware, and shareware, as well as open-source software, available for download online.

Surveillance

Setting up surveillance cameras to be viewed over the Web is nearly a plug-and-play operation, provided you have the necessary IP addresses to support the camera or Web servers. This technology allows, for example, monitoring of your home or office while away or, say, checking on your summer house while you are at home.

Business owners can set up cameras at their place of work to monitor events at the office or keep tabs while away.

Assessing Internet Service Plans

Two things are necessary to establish home access to the Internet: at least one Internet-capable computer on your network and the purchase of an Internet service plan from an Internet service provider (ISP). What plans are available will vary somewhat by geography (with suburban and rural areas having fewer options than urban ones), the communication media you want to use, and the options put forth by your ISP.

Some critical plan features include the following:

- Internet speed
- Customer service support
- Email addresses
- Price
- Equipment provided by ISP
- Nature of IP address provided-static or dynamic
- Complimentary Wi-Fi access
- Transmission media used
- Webpage hosting

How to Get Internet Connectivity

To connect your computer to the Internet, you must choose from the service-plan options available in your area. Once you have evaluated the connection plans and media options in your area, and have selected an ISP, review some of the following considerations below for guidelines on how to set up Internet access.

Using Dial-Up

Dial-up is, for the most part, obsolete from a speed perspective, but in some rural areas, it is the only available low-cost Internet-connection option. When connecting your computer using dial-up over a plain old telephone service (POTS) line, there are three common scenarios:

- Hooking up a computer or laptop with a built-in modem

- Using an external dial-up modem connected via a USB port
- Using a modem that will connect to a 9-pin serial port.

Using Cables

A popular Internet-connection choice in many areas is cable. In fact, your home or small office may already have a cable connection for television service, making the addition of a cable modem to the mix fairly simple. Cable Internet service is high speed-much better than that offered by dial-up. In addition, many cable-based packages bundle increased television channels for viewing and Internet phone service.

Using Wi-Fi

Connecting wirelessly to the Internet is fairly simple, but your network must include a gateway or router designed for wireless connections. In addition, any computers on your network must have Wi-Fi capabilities built-in or, in the case of a laptop or notebook computer, a slot for a wireless Wi-Fi card.

If your computer or workstations are not configured for Wi-Fi, fear not. There are hosts of manufacturers making devices to support wireless connections—essentially, these are portable wireless NICs that can be plugged into either an Ethernet port or a USB port.

Using DSL

Using DSL to connect to the Internet over standard phone lines has an advantage of accessing the internet are higher speeds than the dial-up option (assuming you live in an area where DSL service is available). Moreover, whereas a dial-up connection relies upon the audio/analog band on a phone line, data on a DSL Internet connection passes over the wire pair at a frequency that is higher-meaning that users can still use their phone lines while at the same time using the Internet (and, by extension, keep your Internet connection live 24/7).

Chapter 9: Virtualization Architecture and Cloud computing

Cloud computing refers to the delivery of IT resources via the internet as per the demand. It is normally implemented on a pay-as-you-go pricing basis. The concept of cloud computing seeks to offer a solution to users' needs of IT infrastructure at a low cost.

Essence of Cloud Computing

For small as well as big IT companies that still rely on traditional methods to operate primarily require a server to carry out their different tasks. The setting up of a server room requires skilled personnel, different servers, modems, switches, and lots of other networking resources-plus a lot more of other non-IT requirements that contribute to the completeness of a working office.

Traditional methods require a lot of human input, expensive equipment, and a lot of other logistical necessities. These things require large sums of money. In order to set up a fully functional server, the organization or individual must be willing to break the bank. However, that is no longer thanks to the concept of cloud computing. Cloud computing helps individuals to cut down on infrastructure costs by eliminating the need for the purchase of expensive equipment and spending a lot of funds on hired personnel for the administration and management of IT resources.

Characteristics of Cloud Computing

- Cloud computing operates in a distributed computing environment. This makes resource sharing to happen quickly.
- Cloud computing minimizes the chances of infrastructural failure due to the existence of many servers. This makes it a more reliable infrastructure for IT operations.
- Cloud computing allows for large-scale, on-demand provision of IT resources without the need for engineers and many other professionals that would otherwise come in handy.
- Cloud computing enables multiple users to share resources and work more efficiently by sharing the same infrastructure.
- Cloud computing eliminates physical location or distance concerns since users can access systems and resources regardless of their geographic location.
- Maintaining cloud computing applications is easier since they do not need to be installed on each user's computer.
- Cloud computing reduces the operating cost of an organization since it eliminates the organization's need to set up its own infrastructure-this turns out to be quite an expensive undertaking for most organizations. Besides, it allows an organization to only pay for a service or resource when needed.

- Cloud computing allows for pay-per-use mode for different services. It is a convenient way to use, especially when a user needs to use a resource only once.

Cloud Computing in Practice

Instead of installing a whole suite of costly software for every employee's computer, it is possible to have just a single application where all users can log in and access the resources they need. The application lets users access a web-based service that holds all the applications that are required for the execution of their tasks. Remote servers will do everything while being managed and administered by a third party. This is cloud computing.

In cloud computing, local computers are not concerned with much of the heavy lifting. Remote servers do the heavy lifting-running of even the most sophisticated software and storage of bulky files. These minimize users' hardware and software demands. Even a not so expensive can run a cloud computing interface software. Also, cloud computing eliminates the need to purchase most software applications since they can be accessed via the cloud.

Virtualization

Virtualization is a process by which a virtual version of some actual thing is created. In computing, this may involve virtualization of an operating system, network resources, server, storage device or even a desktop.

Technically, we can refer to virtualization as a technique that permits the sharing of one instance of a physical resource or application among multiple users or groups.

The technique involves the assignment of a logical name to physical storage of a given resource or application and offering a pointer to the specific resource or application as is required.

Types of Virtualization

The following are the different categories of virtualization.

- **Server Virtualization:** When virtual machine manager (VMM)—virtual machine software—is directly installed on the server then the process is referred to as server virtualization.

  Why Server Virtualization?

  Server virtualization is essential because it is possible to subdivide a physical server into multiple servers on a demand basis, and also for load balancing.

- **Storage Virtualization:** This is the process that involves the grouping of multiple physical storage devices in a network so that they appear like a single storage device. Software applications are also used for the implementation of storage virtualization.

  Why storage virtualization?

  This is crucial for recovery and back-up reasons.

- **Operating System Virtualization:** In this case, the virtual machine software (VMM) is installed directly on the operating system of the host machine. Unlike in hardware virtualization, VMM is not installed on the hardware.

  Why operating system virtualization?

  Operating system virtualization comes in handy when there is a need to test applications on a different operating system platform.

- **Hardware Virtualization:** In hardware virtualization, the virtual machine software is installed directly on the hardware system. The hypervisor is charged with the responsibility of controlling and monitoring the memory, processor and hardware resources. We can install different operating systems on the system and use it to run a lot of other applications—after the virtualization of the hardware system.

  Why hardware virtualization?

  Hardware virtualization is largely important for server platforms since the control of virtual machines is not as difficult as the control of a physical server.

Virtualization in Cloud Computing

Virtualization is a greatly potent concept in cloud computing. Normally, in cloud computing, users need to share resources available in the clouds. For instance, applications and files are some of the sharable resources that may be stored in the clouds. With virtualization, users are provided with a platform that making sharing of such resources a practical experience.

The primary goal of virtualization is to offer applications with their standard versions to users in the clouds. When new application versions are released, users look up to a software developer for the new release. This is possible but may turn out to be quite a hectic affair if all users have to download the new version from a central server. To resolve that issue, virtualized servers and software can be maintained by third parties at fee, but cloud users can efficiently access the new software releases.

In summary, virtualization primarily means running several operating systems on one machine that share all hardware resources.

This technique is hugely helpful because it makes it possible to pool network resources and share them with different users conveniently and at less cost.

Components of a Server Computer

The following are the main components of a server computer:

- Storage drives
- Motherboard
- Processor
- Network connection
- Video cards
- Memory
- Power supply

Virtualization Software

The following are the most common popular virtualization software:

- VM Ware Fusion
- VM Ware Workstation
- Parallels Desktop
- Oracle Virtualization
- QEMU
- Microsoft Hyper-V
- Redhat Virtualization
- Veertu-for MAC
- Apple-Boot Camp

Three Basic Kinds of Cloud Services

Cloud computing provides on-demand cloud services to users via the internet. Some of the popular cloud services are:

1. Amazon Web Services
2. Microsoft Azure
3. Google Cloud

Public Clouds vs. Private Clouds

A public cloud hosting solution differs from a private cloud hosting primarily on how either of the two solutions is managed.

Public Cloud Services

A public cloud hosting solution means that user data is stored and managed by a cloud provider. Providers of cloud services that are responsible for the maintenance of data centers are filled with their clients' important data. Many people favor the option of public cloud hosting solution because it is more pocket-friendly as far as management is concerned. However, there are a few people who feel that the safety and security of data in a public cloud are at a higher risk of being compromised. However, the responsibility bestowed upon the cloud provider, from a business and legal point of view, may just be enough motivation to guarantee the security of their clients' data security and safety better.

Private Cloud Services

Private cloud hosting solution means that the responsibility for the maintenance and management of a cloud service lies within a given organization's own arrangement and authority. A private cloud hosting solution is also referred to as enterprise or internal cloud. An organization or enterprise hosts its own cloud service behind a firewall. Though the safety and security of data may be provided at a higher level than it is done at the public cloud hosting solutions, the infrastructural requirements may just prove too costly. It also requires the employment of highly skilled personnel to manage the cloud. This amounts to increased operational costs for an enterprise or organization.

Chapter 10:
Network Troubleshooting

Effective network management must address all issues pertaining to the following:

- Hardware
- Administration and end-user support
- Software
- Data management

Hardware Management and Maintenance

Hardware maintenance can be performed as per the following routines and considerations:

Cleaning

Every two weeks, clean all network equipment. Doing so will help keep your equipment cool and make other maintenance tasks easier to perform. When cleaning, dust the equipment, shelves, and nearby areas. A small vacuum should be used to vacuum keyboards and the computer vent and fan openings. Additionally, you should use the vacuum to gently suck dust out of removable media drives. Unused wall jacks and empty equipment jacks in dust-prone environments can be vacuumed on occasion as well.

For printers and plotters, follow the manual instructions for cleaning print heads on inkjets and vacuuming paper dust from laser printers. Monitors can be wiped down with eye-glass cleaning solutions and glasses-cleaning cloths.

Performing Inspections

Keeping a close eye on the condition of all hardware is essential. For this reason, you should inspect all hardware at least once per month. This inspection should include the following:

- Make sure cooling vents are not blocked or excessively dusty.
- Listen to and feel the vents to make sure cooling fans are operating.
- Sniff the area. When power supplies and other parts are near failing, they may emit an odd odor from excessive heating. A burnt smell means trouble is imminent or has already occurred.
- Check all power cables, peripheral cables, and network cables for tightness in their sockets.
- Check all power cables, peripheral cables, and network cables for fraying or other damage.
- Check the server area for proper operation of heating, venting, and cooling systems to be sure they are operable- even if those systems are not needed at the time of the inspections.

Upgrading Firmware

"Firmware" refers to any program that is resident in a chip. For example, a computer's BIOS is firmware. Sometimes, maker's release updates for firmware to fix flaws or to enable the equipment to work with some newly released hardware device or operating-system upgrade. You should check the manufacturer's Web site or help desk for all network equipment at least quarterly to determine whether any firmware upgrades are available for your equipment.

If so, be sure to adhere to the maker's instructions to the letter for loading new firmware and firmware updates. Firmware loads often require low-level booting from a DOS or maintenance disk, although some will be compatible with the computer's operating system.

Upgrading Hardware

Two factors drive hardware upgrades:

- Performance issues due to changes in applications or the addition of new applications may necessitate a hardware upgrade or the addition of new features that are linked to the hardware's capability or capacity. For example, adding memory and installing an additional hard drive for more file space are typical upgrades performed to support those changes.

- You may opt to upgrade hardware on a purely optional basis-for example, adding a bigger monitor, higher-quality sound card, a TV card, or a similar device.

Repairing Hardware

As the person responsible for the network, you must assess your willingness and ability to perform hardware repairs-before a hardware component stops working. To that end, you should go through your entire hardware inventory and determine the following:

- Is the equipment still under warranty? If so, take advantage of that warranty in the event the equipment stops working.

- Would it be more cost-effective to simply replace a piece of hardware if it breaks? Given the high cost of technical labor, repairing a low-cost item, such as a printer that can be replaced for $50, may not be justified. It might even be best to replace rather than repair PCs purchased for less than $600 if you've used them for more than 10 months. Don't get me wrong: I am not advocating short equipment life cycles or unnecessarily adding to scrap piles.

For big-ticket items, you may want to transfer the repair risk to someone else by arranging for service and support contracts-assuming your budget can support this.

Network Troubleshooting

Network trouble-shooting refers to all the measures and techniques assembled to identify, diagnose and resolve network issues. The process is systematic and primarily seeks to restore normalcy to the functionality of a computer network.

Network administrators are charged with the responsibility of identifying network problems and repairing it with the aim of ensuring a smooth run of operations in the network. They also do whatever it takes to ensure that the network is operating at optimal levels.

The following are just a few of the many computer network troubleshooting processes:

- Configuration and reconfiguration of switches, routers or any other network component.
- Identifying any network issues and figuring out a way to fix it.
- Installation and repair of network cables as well as Wi-Fi devices.
- Getting rid of malware from the network.
- Getting firmware devices up-to-date.
- Installation and uninstallation of software as is necessary.

Network troubleshooting can be done manually or as an automated task-especially when it has to do with network software applications. Network diagnostic software is a valuable tool when it comes to the identification of network issues that may not be easy to detect with the human eye.

Network troubleshooting includes both hardware troubleshooting and software troubleshooting.

Hardware Troubleshooting

This is a form of troubleshooting that takes care of issues with hardware components. It may include:

- Removal of faulty or damaged RAM, hard disk or NIC
- Dusting of computer and other network devices-dust accumulation sometimes leads to malfunctioning of devices
- Tightening of cables that connect different network components
- Updating or installation of important hardware drivers

Hardware troubleshooting begins with the discovery of a given hardware issue, the cause and, finally, taking the necessary remedial action.

Summary of Network Management

Large networks often have one or more staff members dedicated exclusively to performing network administrative tasks. For smaller networks, the manager must wear various hats and perform multiple roles to support the network. Over time, he or she must rise to the level of journeyman-or at least experienced apprentice-to be successful. Primary or routine network-administrative tasks fall into one of the following categories:

- Administering and supporting end-users
- Adding workstations and peripheral devices
- Maintaining system-wide documentation

Maintaining System-Wide Documentation

Maintaining system-wide documentation might seem like a task you could skip, but you should not. Without complete documentation, a lot of person-hours can be wasted when something goes wrong, or when you are trying to add hardware to a server or applications to network hosts or workstations. Regrettably, for some technicians and network managers, checking the documentation prior to making system changes is not a priority one as it should be. Good documentation practices are not a bane because they take time; they are a benefit to the network manager with little time to waste.

Network documentation should include all operation and maintenance booklets as well as manuals for all the hardware.

Administering and Supporting End-Users

As the network administrator, you will likely be responsible for administering and supporting end-users. Examples of tasks you'll need to perform may include the following:

- Vetting new users for security purposes
- Adding, deleting, and changing end-user accounts
- Creating and administering group, role-based, and individual access controls
- Providing technical support
- Adding workstations and peripheral devices

Adding Workstations & Peripheral Devices

There will likely be times when some software-based administrative chores must be completed in order to add new workstations and peripheral devices to the network. Examples are hardcoding an IP address into a new workstation or printer or attaching a new printer to a print server's queue. In addition, users may need to be assigned rights to access new equipment such as printers, along with access passwords for new workstations on the network. For more information, consult the documentation provided with the new equipment and your own documentation of necessary steps from previous changes.

Software Troubleshooting

Software entails a set of measures for scanning, recognizing, diagnosing, and offering solutions to issues with software in the network. It includes issues with network operating systems, diagnostic software as well as software applications installed on individual network computers.

Cable Troubleshooting

Cabling offers a physical connection between network components. Cables are prone to physical interference. As a result, there may result in disruption of connection due to external pressure. They may get damaged, too. When such interference occurs, a lot of issues may arise since interference with cables means direct interference to data transmission. Thus, cable issues always lead to communication lapse since data transmission is hampered.

As a network administrator, it is necessary to identify cable issues and be in a position to offer quick fixes, so that network activities are not interfered with, at least not for long durations.

Wireshark Short Guide

This is a free, open-source software that is used to analyze network traffic in real time. It is an important tool for network security experts as well as administrators. It helps in network troubleshooting for issues that include latency issues, dropped packets, and malicious activities on networks. You need deep networking knowledge to effectively use Wireshark. Wireshark users need to be well-versed with the TCP/IP concept; be capable of reading and interpreting packet headers; understand the process of routing, DHCP and port forwarding, among other things.

How Does Wireshark Work?

Wireshark captures network traffic and quickly converts into a form that is human readable. This helps network administrators to keep track of the nature and amount of network traffic.

To avoid dealing with so much unnecessary traffic, capture filters collect the kind of traffic that is explicitly defined by the network administrator.

Wireshark has features that enable it to make baseline statistics so as to filter what is 'abnormal' from the 'normal.'

Conclusion

A comprehensive understanding of the basic networking concepts is a cornerstone in the pursuit for a fulfilling experience in a rather complex field of computer networking. With a brief yet precise and friendly introduction to networking, every committed learner sets off with an urge to learn more. The first chapter stands out as a package of networking basics that puts the reader on course to understanding more complex networking concepts with ease and convenience. Simple knowledge about the different types of networks, the OSI reference model, peer-to-peer network architectures and network components briefly, but briefly familiarizes a reader about what they should expect as far as networking is concerned.

It is not necessarily for computer network experts (and networking expert wannabes) to take an interest in the networking concept. Network users, who only need the technical know-how of maneuvering around computer networks of different kinds for their personal needs, also have the rare opportunity to equip themselves with knowledge on the technicalities of what they deal with from time to time — the computer network.

For networking enthusiasts, it is no secret that a toddler needs to crawl before effectively getting up on their feet, taking a slight step before hitting the road with total confidence. It is no doubt that this book comprehensively guides the reader through the basics of computer networking by offering a beginner-friendly tutorial on network setup and configuration by first introducing the requisite networking concepts.

To sum up the good start, a few more or less advanced topics of network management and security, the Internet, and virtualization in cloud computing, awaken the reader to a vivid sight of the interesting future in networking study experience.

Made in the USA
Columbia, SC
20 July 2021